A LIFE CHA
AS YOU

Journal therapy is a remark........................w horizons in your life. This ....ways you different kinds of journals and how they can be used for specific results, how to reread and reinterpret your journal as your life evolves, and how other people have achieved self-growth and solved problems through their personal writings. Learn how to write:

- Dialogues—to work through difficult emotions
- Character sketches—as calling cards for your sub-personalities
- Lists—for clarifying thoughts and finding solutions
- Meditative writing—to open up your consciousness
- Topics du Jour—to solve work and career problems
- And many other journal techniques.

From a leading expert in the field, here is all the information you need to begin a dynamic journey to greater insight—to conquer the most important issues in your life.

"A JOY . . . GOOD STUFF! A lively portrait of what it's like to grow along with a journal."
— Henriette Klauser, author of *Writing on Both Sides of the Brain*

"JUST THE RIGHT BOOK BY A MASTER TEACHER to inspire and guide all those interested in personal growth through creative self reflection."
— Strephon Kaplan-Williams
author of *The Jungian-Senoi Dreamwork Manual*

"ONE OF A KIND! Using charm and wit and dozens of adventurous stories, Kay Adams has given us the definitive book on journal writing. JOURNAL TO THE SELF is a must-read for everyone interested in recovery and self-growth."
— Bob Trask
founder of ARAS Foundation and president of Learning Lab

JOURNAL
TO THE
SELF

▼

22 PATHS TO
PERSONAL
GROWTH

Kathleen Adams, M.A.

WARNER BOOKS

A Time Warner Company

The unexamined life is not worth living.

—Socrates

Copyright © 1990 by Kathleen Adams
All rights reserved.

Warner Books, Inc., 1271 Avenue of the Americas, New York, NY 10020

 A Time Warner Company

Cover design by Mario Pulice
Book design by Richard Oriolo

Printed in the United States of America

First Printing: January 1990

10 9 8 7 6 5

Library of Congress Cataloging-in-Publication Data

Adams, Kathleen, 1951–
  Journal to the self : 22 paths to personal growth/Kathleen
Adams.
      p.   cm.
  Includes bibliographical references.
  ISBN 0-446-39038-0
  1. Self-actualization (Psychology)   2. Diaries—Authorship.
I. Title.
BF637.S4A35   1990
158'.1—dc20
                                      89-22482
                                      CIP

Contents

CONTENTS

. . . And then she remembered. She, Princess Ariana, first daughter of King Damien of Vadarado, was lost in the Land of Zin, in a most improbable cave, on a far-flung and storm-drenched night.

"Zeus," she muttered (to herself, as there was no one in the cave). "Whenever *shall* I learn to mind my lessons?"

"When the teacher is ready, the student shall appear," sang a melodious voice, as silken as a teardrop.

Ariana whirled around in amazement. "Why, that's the silliest thing I've ever heard!"

—Kathleen Adams
Ariana and the Goddess of Zin

Lovingly dedicated to my students,
who have fulfilled the Goddess's prophecy.
Let us travel the journey together.

ACKNOWLEDGMENTS

If love's the greatest gift of all, each day of my life is Christmas, for I am blessed with the love and support of several large families. I am profoundly grateful to each.

My first family spills merrily across four generations and ten decades. Thomas Wolfe said, "You can't go home again," but he didn't grow up with Dale and Theda Adams on Estes Court. Their door is always open and their hearts are, too; they have staunchly affirmed my potential from the time I was a tot. From the oldest (90) to the youngest (2), my entire family supports me unconditionally. Now, that's a blessing! Thanks, Mom,

ACKNOWLEDGMENTS

Dad, Susie, Cindy, Granddad Bill, Goggie, Jessica, Jake, Ricki, Amy, Mike, Leo, Billie, Ray, and the souls of Aunt Katy and Becky. I love you!

My second family is the faculty, administration, and student body at Boulder Graduate School (Boulder, Colorado), where I teach, study, laugh, cry, work, and play. Only in my wildest fantasy did I imagine a graduate program in psychotherapy based on the dual trilogy of body/mind/spirit and theory/skills/experience. It's alive and well and living at BGS, and I'm proud to be a graduate.

My third family is my family of wonderful, giving, caring, loving friends. My sisterhood of writers and other professionals—including Sher Long, Normandi Ellis, C. J. Pollara, Sarah Hoskin, Jasmin Cori, Cathleen Huffman, Lyn Merriman, Diana Keck, Dr. Lynn White, Dr. Kathryn Fentress, and especially Marta Hedde—provided invaluable feedback on the manuscript at critical stages. For my Akasha group—Thia Walser, Laura Olsen, Andrea Hilgert, and Jean Jameson—I give thanks. Special appreciation goes to my poet friend, Lois Bay, for permission to use her copyrighted poem, "Windbreak." Mrs. Wilma Long graciously loaned me her beautiful home while I crashed out the first draft of the book on a long winter's night. My friend Joannah invited my right brain to Stone Walls, Vermont. Linda Barclay of Dove Literary not only sold the book in amazingly short order but also handled the business details with crisp efficiency, and Beth Lieberman, my editor at Warner, offered reassurance, insight, and gentle support throughout the process. LeeAnne Lewis believed in me when I needed it most. Carl Kallansrud held my vision when I got tired and laid it down.

Students in the Journaling as a Therapeutic Tool classes at BGS and Write On! workshops in Denver provided most of the examples you'll find in these pages; to respect their privacy, I have fictionalized their names and certain circumstances unless

ACKNOWLEDGMENTS

they directed otherwise. Their contributions are what make the pages of this book come alive.

Several of my mentors also deserve thanks. John Klug, president of Continental Communications Group, runs a first-rate publishing company and helped mold my writing during the six years I served as his editorial vice president. Eiko Michi and her Transformational Journal Workshop were turning points in my own journal journey. Bob Trask, president of the ARAS Foundation, encouraged me to "do my life's work" and taught me how to teach. Dr. Lynn Ward White, former chairperson of the psychology and counseling department at BGS, has the uncanny ability to see the vision behind my doodles. To John, Eiko, Bob, and Lynn, my profound thanks. How different my life would be had I not encountered you!

PREFACE

Journal therapy—the use of the journal, or diary, to facilitate holistic mental health and self-reliance—can trace its roots back as far as 10th-century Japan, when ladies of the Heian court wrote reflections on life and love in "pillow books." Nearly a millennium later, Anne Frank, in one of history's classic underestimations, confided to herself: "It's an odd idea for someone like me to keep a diary, because it seems to me that neither I—nor, for that matter, anyone else—will be interested in the unbosomings of a thirteen-year-old schoolgirl."

Dr. Ira Progoff has been the leader of journal therapy devotees since 1966, when his Intensive Journal Workshop™ debuted as an outcome of his model of holistic depth psychology. Dr. Progoff's beautifully crafted weekend workshop offers participants a glimpse into their own transpersonal natures, a direct experience with what he calls the "knowledge beyond understanding . . . that comes to us at depth."

I am sometimes asked how my system of journal therapy differs from Dr. Progoff's. I believe it is a matter of approach rather than philosophy, for I feel very strongly that everyone writing and teaching about journal therapy today holds a collective vision of the individual's self-knowledge and spiritual awakening.

At a strictly pragmatic level, the Intensive Journal™ method is physically different from the "smorgasbord" approaches you'll find in this book. The Intensive Journal™ is characterized by its three-ring notebook segregated into six major "dimensions," or sections, and specific suggestions on what and how to write in each dimension. While this approach has many strengths (see chapter 4, "Choices," for a discussion), some students who begin their journal journey with an Intensive Journal™ workshop have difficulty organizing their thoughts and feelings into its suggested structure. On the other hand, the journal method presented in this book is nothing if not eclectic; there is no structure or form save that of the individual's choosing.

At a more theoretical level, my training and experience lie in the humanistic therapies—those schools of therapeutic thought which hold as tasks the development of self-esteem, the building of healthy boundaries, and the art of knowing oneself. The goal of humanistic journal therapy is a healthy relationship with self, and this book is intended to facilitate this development. As this healthy relationship evolves, the journey continues toward a relationship with the transpersonal Self—that part of each of us that transcends time and space, our link with that which is known by many names: God, Spirit, the Universe,

PREFACE

Infinite Intelligence, the Tao, Higher Self, Christ Consciousness, the All. Dr. Progoff's Intensive Journal™ works extensively with this level of spiritual and transpersonal awakening.
And so you can begin to see that the two approaches, rather than
being separate and different from one another, are actually
points on a blending continuum.

Among the theorists who have influenced my work are Carl
Rogers, Abraham Maslow, Carl Jung, Milton Erickson, Roberto Assagioli, Virginia Satir, Fritz Perls, Jacquelyn Small, and
of course, Ira Progoff himself. Yet the synthesis of these ideas
remains my own, and just as there are no wrong questions, so
are there no right answers. If my philosophical world view does
not correspond with your own, then take whatever liberties you
will. For there is ultimately only one truth, although there are
a myriad of ways to express it.

Because I was a writer long before I was a therapist, this book
approaches journal writing from the standpoint of *techniques*—
different ways to write that will not only add variety but can also
help maximize the clarity and effectiveness of the journal. The
Dialogue and Steppingstones techniques come directly from Dr.
Progoff's work, and I am grateful for his kind permission to
share my interpretations of them. The remaining techniques are
refinements of literary and therapeutic styles that lend themselves to reflective writing. Although I certainly can't take
credit for "originating" anything as pragmatic as a description
or a list, the three techniques that some closest to being original
are Captured Moments, Lists of 100, and Topics du Jour.

In its very essence, journal therapy is a bridge into first our
own humanity, and then our own spirituality. The road
stretches out before us, and our ultimate task is the journey.

SECTION 1

THE 79¢
THERAPIST

▼

INTRODUCTION

A friend of mine went on a three-month hiking trip through Nepal, and even though she was an experienced mountaineer with years of training behind her, she was required to attend six weeks of ground school.

What could she possibly learn in hiking ground school?

"Oh, everything," she casually replied. "You know. The basics."

This section is like hiking ground school. Whether you're an old journal pro or a novice, you'll find the basics in here.

Like why write a journal, and what sorts of things you can

learn from it, and what the "rules" are, and how to manage your journal entries.

There's a chapter on ways to write a journal if you don't have time, and a chapter by men who write journals, for men who might want to.

You know. The basics.

Happy hiking!

1

THE 79¢
THERAPIST

In moments of ecstasy, in moments of despair the journal remains an impassive, silent friend, forever ready to coach, to confront, to critique, to console. Its potential as a tool for holistic mental health is unsurpassed.

—Write On! workshop advertisement

For nearly 30 years I have had the same therapist. This therapist is available to me 24 hours a day and hasn't gone on vacation in almost three decades. I have called upon my therapist at three in the morning, on my wedding day, on my lunch break, on a cold and lonely Christmas, on a Bora Bora beach, and in the dentist's reception room.

I can tell this therapist absolutely anything. My therapist listens silently to my most sinister darkness, my most bizarre fantasy, my most cherished dream. And I can say all this in any way that I want: I can scream, whimper, thrash, wail, rage, exult, foam, celebrate. I can be funny, snide, introspective, accusatory, sarcastic, helpless, brilliant, sentimental, cruel, profound, caustic, inspirational, opinionated, or vulgar.

My therapist accepts all of this and more without comment, judgment, or reprisal.

Best of all, this therapist keeps a detailed record of all of our work together, so that I have on my bookshelf a chronology of my life—my loves, my pains, my wins, my wounds, my growth, my transformation.

Has this cost a fortune? you ask. Not at all. My therapist doesn't want payment.

My therapist is my journal, which I write in spiral notebooks, obtainable for under a dollar in any city in the country. That's why I call my journal "the 79¢ therapist."

MY JOURNAL JOURNEY

My own journal journey began when I was ten. Envious of my older sister's nightly retreat into her locked diary, I waited impatiently for the time when I, too, would have a life sufficiently unpredictable that it merited chronicle. My favorite gift my tenth Christmas was a five-year diary that allotted six lines for each day's entry.

In 1962, the life-style of the average suburban sixth-grader wasn't particularly glamorous. Some days it was a struggle to fill up even six lines:

> It snowed. I had to wear boots to school. I hate wearing boots to school! They're UGGHHHH!!!!!

Or:

> Mr. Mason was sick. We had a substitute. She was boring. Barbie M. and I ate lunch together.

And so one day I recorded not what *had* happened in school that day, but what I *wished* had happened:

Jack T. was waiting for me at the corner. He carried my books. He said he's loved me since 4th. He asked me to go steady. I said ok but only if it's secret.

And then:

Tommy S. walked me home from school and boy was Jack mad!!!!! He said he won't go steady anymore unless it's not secret. I don't know who I like better.

As I warmed to my fantasy life, the cast of supporting players (all plucked from Mr. Mason's classroom) grew, and the plots began to take intricate twists and turns. Not only was my own fictional love life logged for posterity, but also scandals involving my school chums popped up with alarming regularity.

The inevitable ethical dilemma (What if somebody reads it and believes it?) and the nagging literary fear (What if somebody reads it and doesn't?) finally cut short my budding career as a soap opera scriptwriter; I destroyed my first diary and vowed not to write another.

But I did. And another, and another after that.

I have now been writing journals and diaries for 27 years, and I'm happily hooked for life.

As it turned out, soap opera scriptwriting wasn't in my professional future. But writing was, and so was psychotherapy. And then, at last, they married.

Journals.

Since that happy day, I have taught and lectured about journal writing and its applications as a tool for personal growth and self-discovery, both to therapists and to individuals who want to learn how to heal themselves. It has been, and is, a consummate joy. I am in love with my work.

RACHEL'S JOURNAL JOURNEY

Perhaps the most rewarding and fascinating part of journal therapy is this: it spreads out before you in black and white the contents of the heart, mind, and soul. You simply cannot appreciate how healing and powerful this is until you have experienced it.

Take, for example, eight weeks in the life of Rachel, an adult child of an alcoholic father, whose husband had filed for divorce unexpectedly and without explanation. Rachel began her journal journey in the summer of 1988:

> June 30. So! Here I am writing in my journal, feeling self-conscious. A new pen and notebook do not a journal make. . . .
>
> July 1. Hmmmmm. Fighting the urge to rip out last night's entry to "do over." But last night was last night and cannot be done over. Be here now!

It didn't take Rachel long to address the painful issues common to Adult Children of Alcoholics (ACAs):

> July 3. Why should I be afraid to ask what I possibly couldn't know? I never realized the extent to which the prison of not knowing has contributed to my aloneness.
>
> July 4. I don't want to write these words. But I have already written them, and they are true. And lightning didn't strike. But it is so painful to be vulnerable.

Despite her early discomfort, Rachel soon found herself using her journal to take inventory of her life:

> July 6. So today is your birthday. It's been quite a year, wouldn't you say?

July 9. Today I had an experience that has shot huge gaping holes in everything that I believe to be true. . . .

Rachel found that her present-day feelings of discomfort and depression echoed an earlier time, which she explored in a Steppingstones essay:

July 14. It was a time when I felt like a nobody and when I lost everything I thought was mine—including people I had counted on, home, as well as my own heart. . . .

With some of her ACA issues in focus, Rachel used Unsent Letters to clarify her feelings about her father's recovery from alcoholism:

July 16. Dear Dad: I want you to get help but I don't believe you will. . . . Take the plunge. You have nothing more to lose.

Three weeks into the process, Rachel noticed a shift in her relationship with her journal:

July 18. I just reviewed the last few entries in comparison to the first. I must feel more comfortable—my handwriting is messier! Hello, journal!

The "disidentification" process continued with a list of "100 Things I Am Not." Rachel followed up with:

July 20. I know now I will not die—knowledge I previously had in my head but not in my heart—and I will stay with this sadness as best I can.

This shift in awareness allowed her to verbalize long-denied anger and resentments:

July 28. I'm sick of it!! I'm sick of being in recovery and still feeling unclean and dishonest. I'm sick of sadness and pain. I'm sick of trying so hard and still not getting it.

And I hate this journal for pointing it out to me *all the time*. I hate you, journal!!!

And as if this entry were the "labor pains" of her soul, the very next entry logged a dream:

August 1. I am pregnant and give birth to a girl. The labor is swift. . . .

In a whimsical dialogue with her cat, Rachel received cogent feline advice:

August 2. CAT: Hey—loosen up. Be more like me—live in the moment, without judgment, get love where you can and purr a lot.
RACHEL: Yeah—well, it sounds good—but . . .
CAT: Those endless buts! Let's go play!

An entry logging "current events" opened the door to more exploration of her anger:

August 7. Today I found out the divorce will be finalized in September. I feel angry about it—the whole sense of its being done *to* me—as if the divorce is an entity of its own, going on about its way without taking my feelings into account.

In a Stream of Consciousness spiral, Rachel began with the word "Self" and circled her way around and around until she was finally able to break loose with the phrase "get angry," which she did in a journal dialogue with her husband. Her anger and hurt expressed at last, Rachel found a curious calm in an Unsent Letter to her husband:

August 15. The time has come to say good-bye. You're right—part of me has been attached to the pain and energy connected to the unresolved status of our relationship. I'll miss you. . . . As I write this, I realize I never had the chance to say good-bye and that's been part of my struggle to let go. So I use this time and space to say good-bye, to say I forgive you and wish you the best. . . . Adios. Good-bye. Love, Rachel.

Tender with harvested pain, Rachel ended this eight-week leg of her journey with a list entitled "Things I Am Grateful For."

We live out our lives in cycles. The tides ebb and flow. The moon blooms into fullness and recedes. We live a hundred tiny deaths from hour to hour. And as it did with Rachel, each death inevitably leads to rebirth.

YOUR JOURNAL JOURNEY

Every time I begin a class, I ask the students what they want to gain from the experience. We create a list of "collective class goals," which usually includes items such as:

- Get to know myself better
- Learn how to use the journal for problem solving
- Take time for myself
- Record my personal history
- Get over a relationship

After everyone has had an opportunity to contribute to the collective list, I add the last one:

- Have fun!

For the journal journey is not always dreary, heavy, or tumultuous. Sometimes, to be sure, the path is a steep uphill climb; sometimes it seems you're hiking down the Grand Canyon without a burro. But remember that your journal will log your joy just as faithfully as your pain, your laughter with as much expression as your tears, your triumphs in as much detail as your tragedies. Notice the parts of the journal journey that are playful, joyful, and exuberant, and write about them, too. Remember that rainbows are real, even if the pot of gold isn't.

Ready for the journey? There's not much to pack—only a notebook of your choice, a pen or pencil that feels good, and this trail map. If there's anything else that you need, just throw it in your backpack. And away we'll go!

2

THE FRIEND AT THE
END OF THE PEN

A journal is a friendly thing. It's a friendly thing to do.
–Write On! workshop participant

There's a friend at the end of your pen which you can use to help you solve personal or business problems, get to know all the different parts of yourself, explore your creativity, heal your relationships, develop your intuition . . . and much more.

This friend, of course, is your journal. Empty, blank, smooth—a beautiful gift waiting to be unwrapped!

WHY WRITE A JOURNAL?
A DOZEN ANSWERS

1. Discover the writer within you. If you've told yourself for years that writing isn't fun, give it one more chance. You'll find that your journal doesn't care if you spell words correctly, put commas in the proper place, or scribble in the margins. You can draw a picture, write in circles around the page, write big and sloppy or tiny and precise. Journal writing is a near-perfect hobby: inexpensive, always available, no special equipment or skills required, expandable or contractable to fit any time allotment. And for those of you who take care of others at the expense of taking care of yourself (you know who you are!), your journal can be a bottomless well of self-nurturing.

If you've told yourself for years that you can't write, give *yourself* one more chance, too. When you replace a "performance" expectation with an "enjoyment" expectation, you're likely to surprise yourself at how much better you like what you write!

2. Keep a record for the future of how your life unfolds. It is the nature of the human psyche to move toward wholeness and growth; each of us holds at our core a deep desire to become "more of who we really are." Your journal will serve as scribe throughout the journey of your life, obligingly recording your own uniquely forged path toward individuation, keeping an accurate log of the uphill trudge, the view from the summit, the ambling strolls through wildflower-strewn meadows, the terrifying descents into the abyss.

There is something very magical about going back into your life and observing it from the vantage point of a month or a year or 10 years later. Your journal will stand as a chronicle of your growth, your hopes, your fears, your dreams, your ambitions, your sorrows, your serendipities.

Leigh was pregnant with her first child when she began her journal journey, and her entries consisted exclusively of letters to her unborn son. "When Tucker is 15 or 16, and we're going through all the teenage trauma," she said, "I want to be able to go back to these journal letters and share them with him. I want my son to know how much his father and I loved him and wanted him even before his birth. Somehow I think that will help to ease any temporary disruption all of us may be experiencing." What a precious gift of communication and understanding!

Many businesspeople who write journals about their corporate or career lives swear by the value of keeping a record of peak and slump times in business. "When sales start falling, I can go back and reconstruct what I did to boost them the last time I was in this cycle," said Roger, a systems design executive. "It's also reassuring to read back through my business journal and realize that nothing lasts forever."

3. Get to know all the different parts of yourself.

Psychologically as well as physically, each of us is made up of many different pieces; we are human jigsaw puzzles. The Italian psychologist Roberto Assagioli called these different parts of ourselves "subpersonalities." Our subpersonalities are like a wardrobe full of mental and emotional costumes; we "dress up" in one or another to fit the changing situations and circumstances of our lives. One of the goals of psychosynthesis, the therapy Assagioli developed as his life's work, is to integrate and synthesize the various subpersonalities into the larger and deeper whole, the Self.

You're undoubtedly familiar with some of your own subpersonalities. Recent literature in the Adult Children of Alcoholics movement identifies several subpersonalities that people who grew up in an alcoholic or other dysfunctional household typically develop. These include the Lost Child (the part of you that wants to hide in a corner when conflict arises), the Scapegoat (the part of you that protests against family chaos by acting out or getting into trouble yourself), the Family Hero (the part of you that wants to be perfect), or the Mascot, Joker, or Comedian (the part of you that tries to distract attention away from family troubles by being comical, cute, or appealing).

If you have children, you undoubtedly have both Loving Parent and Stern Parent subpersonalities. Most of us have some variation of an Inner Critic or Perfectionist subpersonality that unrealistically expects us to do everything without error. Other subpersonalities familiar to many women include Competent Woman, Supermom, the Vamp, Dutiful Daughter, Ms. PMS, the Clinging Vine, Earth Mother, Scared Little Girl, and the High Priestess. Subpersonalities familiar to many men include Weekend Daddy, Marathon Runner, Breadwinner, Armchair Quarterback, Casanova, Scared Little Boy, and Knight in Shining Armor.

There are other subpersonalities with which you may not be very familiar. Assagioli called these the "shadow" subpersonalities, because the light of your own awareness has not yet touched them and allowed them to come forward for recognition and integration. These may be the parts of yourself that deal with anger or fear or sexuality; you may even think that they don't exist at all.

Your journal can serve as a magic mirror into which you can gaze and see reflected back to you the various parts of yourself. And as you come to know and love your many parts, as you learn how your subpersonalities have helped you meet your needs and stay safe, as you learn to ask the gentle questions "How can I help you?" and "What do you need from me?" you will find that more and more of yourself is integrating into your Self.

4. Take advantage of "a friend in need" and a valuable tool in the therapeutic process. Certainly one of the most important uses of the journal is its tremendous potential as a therapeutic tool, whether in a program of counseling with a trained expert or in a self-designed program of personal process.

In 1987 I conducted a study on journaling as a therapeutic tool. Every one of the respondents said that one of the reasons they wrote a journal was because "I can talk to myself on paper and work myself through problems." And 93 percent said that their journals were "valuable tools for self-therapy."

Each respondent listed three words or phrases that described his or her relationship with the journal. Fully 87 percent of the responses described the relationship as a friendly or therapeutic one. Specific words used to describe the journal included: friend, therapist, sounding board, companion, confidant. Another group of words described the journal in terms of the qualities of friendship and/or therapy: close, intimate, trusting, caring, honest, nonjudgmental.

My own experience tells me that when a journal is used in conjunction with a program of therapy, in most cases the client moves through issues more quickly and integrates new learnings more readily. Some therapists and clients agree on journal "homework" to be completed between sessions. If you are currently undergoing counseling, talk to your therapist about incorporating your journal into the work you do together. It will not only help your therapist to be more effective, but there is a two-fold benefit for you, as well: First, you can save yourself both money and time because the journal generally helps to accelerate the therapeutic process. Second, your journal is a valuable tool for empowering you with problem-solving and self-processing skills when your therapeutic relationship is completed.

You may not want to seek the professional services of a therapist or counselor. You may not have the money or the time or a therapist who is available to you. Sometimes the issue you're working with is a short-term, situational problem that doesn't really merit a lengthy counseling relationship.

That's when your journal can really shine. You can learn to act as your *own* therapist, working yourself through problems, coming to new levels of discovery, asking yourself questions and letting yourself answer them.

Jean Jameson, in her paper *The Five Stages of Grief As Experienced in My Journal* (see chapter 20), explained it this way:

> Where would I have been without my journal? It has become the archetypal friend. I have used and abused it more than any person would have tolerated. But it was always there waiting for me; I could say absolutely anything and there was never a judgment, never a criticism. It was totally accepting and totally present; it gave me a chance to be me and demanded nothing in return. I could carry it around with me, snatching bits and pieces of time, and it never wanted more. I could grab it in the middle of the night, and it never asked for less. I could chide it and discount its value and it never took offense. I never had to start over; I never had to apologize. And where else would it have been possible to process a subject as dreary as grief? I wouldn't even expect a friend to listen to the stuff I dumped in my journal. A trip about grief, through grief, including denial, anger, bargaining and depression. No small favor to ask. And my journal took it gladly—welcoming the catharsis—filling up and becoming more in the process. What a blessed gift. What a joyous experience, and it is with me now as I move into acceptance.

5. Heal your relationships. If your relationship conflicts involve people who are active and present in your life, the journal can provide a safe forum in which to ventilate strong feelings that may not be appropriate for direct expression.

In other words, in your journal you can cuss out your boss, scream at your mother, and yell at your spouse to your heart's content. This discharges the emotion and leaves you sane and sensible for an actual conversation, in which you'll likely find yourself able not only to state your wants and needs in an assertive manner but also to listen to the other's point of view, as well.

If you are haunted by what Elisabeth Kübler-Ross calls "unfinished business" with someone who is no longer available to you (through death, abandonment, or simply moving on), your journal can help you sort through the conflict and pain.

Naomi used Unsent Letters, Dialogues, and Lists to come to terms with the painful realization that her alcoholic ex-husband might never stop drinking. Gretchen used Guided Imagery and Captured Moments to soothe the sobbing child inside whose father had "deserted" her by dying when she was eight. Bruce used Steppingstones, Character Sketches, and Perspectives to help resolve his feelings of impotence and anger in relation to "the Company" which fired him three years before his retirement.

Try incorporating journal writing into your family's problem-solving and communication styles. The Marriage Encounter™ seminar promotes a "10-and-10" system for establishing good relationship communication skills: Write a 10-minute "love letter" on a predetermined topic each day, then exchange letters with your spouse or lover and spend another 10 minutes reading and talking about the letters. I often recommend to couples and families that they keep a community or relationship journal in which can be recorded anything that any family member finds difficult or awkward to discuss. It's a sensitive way to open the door to meaningful communication.

6. Access information stored in the subconscious and unconscious minds. Jungian and other transpersonal psychologies teach that the human mind is made up of four parts: conscious, subconscious, unconscious, and superconscious (or collective unconscious). To get an idea of their relationships to each other, imagine yourself on a beach. Closest to you, the waves that crest into the air and crash against the shore can be thought of as your *conscious* mind—that part from which you actively perceive and remember. As you shift your focus a little further in the distance, the water below the surface that builds to form the waves can be considered your *subconscious* mind, where your brain stores memories and information that can be brought up and over to consciousness. Looking even further in the distance, the water that stretches out to the horizon is like your *unconscious* mind; it is vast, and it touches other lands, lives, civilizations, cultures. But if the tides are pulling a certain way, this water can be worked to the subconscious, and then the conscious, level.

The journal is like the moon, emitting a magnetic tug that draws information from your subconscious and unconscious minds and brings it to the surface, where you can work at the conscious level.

7. Access information from your superconscious mind—the collective unconscious or your "Higher Self." Returning to the ocean metaphor, the water that extends down into the depths of the earth is like your superconscious mind. This level has a life and energy all its own; it is home to entire civilizations, and it constantly feeds each of the other levels in turn. It is at this level that you connect with the unity of the ocean and begin to sense that you are indeed one drop of a vast wholeness, blending your individuality with the individualities of infinite other drops to cocreate the All-

That-Is. What has popularly become known as channeling or automatic writing comes from this level of your mind.

8. Explore your dreams in the journal.

Many techniques used in dream therapy (such as Jungian active imagination, Gestalt identification, and Freudian free association) can easily be translated to written form; any technique that you would use for a situation or relationship in your waking life can be used for its dreaming counterpart. Let your journal serve as scrivener as you venture down what Freud called the "royal road to the unconscious."

9. Recognize the symbology of your life and develop your intuition.

Intuition, your "sixth sense," does not communicate to you in the same way as your other five senses; rather, it communicates in symbols and inner sensings. Viewing your life symbolically, as a series of outer events with potential for inner meaning, is at the heart of intuitive living and allows us to "glimpse . . . the reality that there is indeed a link between us all, between us and all living things, between us and the universe," as Dr. Jean Shinoda Bolen states.

Capturing the symbolism in seemingly happenstance events can infuse your life with richness and depth:

> Symbolism in conversation with Sam last night just sunk in. I was so glad to see him—he looked terrific. I said, "Samuel! Here I am trying to talk to you and all I can see is myself in those funky glasses you are wearing!" He took off his glasses and we both laughed. Don't we see ourselves in everyone we talk to!

According to Dr. Bolen, *synchronicities,* those marvelous serendipities of "meaningful coincidence" where outer event and inner meaning are fused, may be like waking dreams: we may each have several of them a day, even if we don't recognize or remember them. In *The Tao of Psychology* she continues, "Synchronicity, like dreams, invites us to participate at the symbolic level, where we sense there is underlying meaning."

Synchronicities, symbols, life metaphors, and miracles are all like four-leaf clovers: You'll never find one if you're not looking. Get into the habit of asking yourself, "How is this situation a metaphor for another part of my life?" or "Where is the symbolism in this?" Then let your intuition answer. (Incidentally, it's a very common experience to feel as if you're "making it up" when you write intuitively.)

10. Maximize time and business efficiency. Many of the most popular speakers on the motivational circuit tout journal writing as one of the best-kept secrets of success. Jim Rohn, an avid keeper of a business journal, says that he once bought an expensive, "very handsome," leather-bound book with gilt-edged blank pages. A friend asked in scorn why he would spend all that money on an empty book. "Why, because I intend to fill it," Jim replied grandly, "with *million-dollar ideas!*"

Contrary to what you might think, the time you spend on a business journal can be very cost-effective. When you're focused, you can accomplish an amazing amount in 15 minutes or less, and you may just find that writing in your business journal is the most productive and profitable time you spend during the day.

11. Explore your creativity. Write a poem. Add some music; sing a song. Doodle out a short story. Paint a picture with words or tempura. Your journal is a forgiving canvas for expressions of creativity that you feared were dead and buried.

Remember when you were a tiny child, drawing mysterious shapes and hieroglyphics with crayons? "That's a cow in the snow," you would proudly proclaim, "and *that* part says, 'I love you, Grandpa.'"

Draw a cow in the snow.

12. Track the cycles, patterns, and trends of your life.
No longer need you be subject to the mercy of your "moods"—
with a little forethought and a commitment to chart yourself for
a few weeks or months, you're likely to find amazing information about your personal patterns. Over time, you'll begin to
notice and plan for your down times, your creative times, your
introspective times.

Are you in recovery for any sort of addictive or compulsive
behavior? Charting is an excellent way to ease your passage
through the difficult stages of recovery. It is virtually impossible
to successfully change long-term habits until the behaviors and
belief systems associated with the habits are isolated and
pinpointed. Once again, the journal can not only serve as an
adjunct therapist/counselor/physician, but it can help soothe
your frayed nerves and frustrated feelings during the recovery
process. As a bonus, you'll be left with a permanent testament
of your mastery over your addiction.

Are you a business executive? You'll love the way the journal
helps you identify the cycles of profitability and productivity
and improve time management.

Do you suffer from PMS? Try charting your cycles in the
journal. After only a few months, you'll probably be able to
pinpoint the days of your cycle when you are most susceptible
to irritability or gloominess—and you can plan your business
and personal life accordingly.

Of course, these aren't the only reasons to write a journal.
Among other things, the journal can help you get (and stay) in
touch with your feelings, develop spontaneity, develop self-
discipline, try on new behaviors and beliefs, imagine your own
possibilities, or make your fantasies real. It doesn't really matter
which reason you choose. Just remember to have fun, try new
things, and enjoy the journey.

TECHNIQUE CROSS-CHECK

Use this handy cross-check to find the techniques that are particularly well suited to your special reasons for writing a journal:

1. Discover the writer within you. All of the techniques can be fun. Experiment until you find the ones you like best. Be sure to read:

"Eight Suggestions for Satisfying Journal Writing" (chapter 3)

"Journals to Go" (chapter 5)

2. Keep a record for the future of how your life unfolds. Try these techniques:

"Captured Moments" (chapter 10)

"Steppingstones" (chapter 14)

"Time Capsule" (chapter 15)

"Topics du Jour" (chapter 16)

3. Get to know all the different parts of yourself. These techniques are particularly useful:

"Character Sketch" (chapter 8)

"Dialogue" (chapter 11)

"Steppingstones" (chapter 14)

"Unsent Letters" (chapter 17)

"Perspectives" (chapter 18)

"Dreams and Imagery" (chapter 19)

4. Take advantage of "a friend in need" and a valuable tool in the therapeutic process. Any of the techniques in section II are useful for working yourself through problems. Use the ones that seem most appropriate. Techniques favored by subjects in the study were:

"Dialogue" (chapter 11)

"Unsent Letters" (chapter 17)
"Dreams and Imagery" (chapter 19)
See also section III, "Putting It All Together."

5. Heal your relationships. Start with:
"Character Sketch" (chapter 8)
"Dialogue" (chapter 11)
"Steppingstones" (chapter 14)
"Unsent Letters" (chapter 17)
"Perspectives" (chapter 18)
See also section III, "Putting It All Together," and chapter 6, "For Men Only."

6. Access information stored in the subconscious and unconscious minds. Try:
"Clustering" (chapter 9)
"Captured Moments" (chapter 10)
"Dialogue" (chapter 11)
"Lists" (chapter 12)
"Stream of Consciousness" (chapter 13)
"Dreams and Imagery" (chapter 19)

7. Access information from your superconscious (or collective unconscious, or "Higher Self") mind. Particularly helpful are:
"Dialogue" (chapter 11; *see* Inner Wisdom Dialogue, p. 118)
"Stream of Consciousness" (chapter 13)
"Dreams and Imagery" (chapter 19)

8. Explore your dreams in the journal. Techniques for do-it-yourself dreamwork included:
"Character Sketch" (chapter 8)
"Clustering" (chapter 9)

"Dialogue" (chapter 11)

"Stream of Consciousness" (chapter 13)

"Perspectives" (chapter 18)

"Dreams and Imagery" (chapter 19)

9. Recognize the symbology of your life and develop your intuition. Deepen your awareness with:

"Springboards" (chapter 7)

"Dialogue" (chapter 11)

"Stream of Consciousness" (chapter 13)

"Dreams and Imagery" (chapter 19)

10. Maximize time and business efficiency. Try:

"Journals to Go" (chapter 5)

"Springboards" (chapter 7)

"Clustering" (chapter 9)

"Lists" (chapter 12)

"Time Capsule" (chapter 15)

"Topics du Jour" (chapter 16)

"Unsent Letters" (chapter 17)

11. Explore your creativity. Have fun with:

"Clustering" (chapter 9)

"Captured Moments" (chapter 10)

"Steppingstones" (chapter 14)

See also the references to poetry and art throughout section II.

12. Track the cycles, patterns, and trends of your life.
These techniques are good:

"Springboards" (chapter 7)

"Steppingstones" (chapter 14)

"Time Capsule" (chapter 15)

"Topics du Jour" (chapter 16)

3

EIGHT SUGGESTIONS
FOR SATISFYING
JOURNAL WRITING

It's wonderful to know there's an area of my life where I don't have to make myself be perfect.

—student of Journaling As a Therapeutic Tool

If you're going to play the game, you have to play by the rules, right? Wrong! When it comes to your journal, there simply *aren't* any rules. This is one of the hardest things for new journalers to accept. Spelling doesn't matter. Grammar doesn't matter. Penmanship doesn't matter; in fact, allowing your handwriting to be however it wants to be is often a barometer of your subconscious process. (You can always tell how angry you are—just check how many pages under the one you're writing on are marked by the indentation of your pen!) Writing every day doesn't matter. Nothing matters except that you're pleased with the results you're getting. And if you're not pleased, try a different technique, schedule, writing instrument, notebook, or approach—until you find something that works for you.

Here's a list of the "Terrible Ten"—the most common "rules" people associate with journal writing. See how many you agree with, even secretly:

1. I should spell all the words correctly and use proper grammar and punctuation.
2. I should write until I get to the bottom of an issue. It isn't okay to quit before it's finished.
3. I should write every day, or at least at regular intervals.
4. My journal shouldn't be messy. I shouldn't cross out words or lines or write things in the margins.
5. My journal should be interesting for other people to read.
6. I shouldn't let *anyone* else read my journal. (Lots of people who believe their journals should be interesting for other people to read also believe this.)
7. I shouldn't say horrible things about people I love, use four-letter words, complain, whine, or get angry.
8. In case I get run over by a truck, I should destroy my diaries periodically to spare my children the pain of finding and reading them.
9. Once I start journal writing, I should stay with it. It should become a lifetime discipline.
10. (Fill in your favorite journal rule)_____

_____

_____

Good news! You can draw a great big **X** through all of those "rules." Because none of them is really a rule of journal writing. In fact, journal writing doesn't have *any* rules. When you're writing in your journal, you can make it up as you go along. Imagine the freedom and possibilities of knowing you can make no mistakes!

I do, however, have some suggestions for satisfying journal writing. These are habits I've developed over the years, because I've found that they work as enhancements to a program of journal self-discovery. Try them out. Then discard any that don't fit for you.

ONE: START WITH AN ENTRANCE MEDITATION

Just about every journal session benefits from a few minutes of focused quieting at the beginning. The purpose of the entrance meditation is to quiet down your head chatter and prime the internal pump. How you choose to enter a journaling session depends a lot on your internal preference for assimilating information. According to Richard Bandler and John Grinder, who developed a psychotherapy known as neurolinguistic programming (NLP), most people are predominantly visual, auditory, or kinesthetic.

If you don't know your own preference, try this experiment: Close your eyes and focus your attention on the memory of a pleasant Christmas. Don't think too much about it; just pick one. Spend a few moments recalling that Christmas. Then open your eyes.

If you *saw* the faces of your loved ones, the softly falling snow, the heap of brightly wrapped presents under the tree, you probably process information well through your *visual* sense.

If you *heard* the Christmas carols, the shrieks of glee from the children, the "Ho, ho, ho!" of Santa, you are likely to prefer an *auditory* way of assimilating information.

If you *felt* the presence of the season, the crispness of the winter air, the affectionate feelings for those around you, then you might be a *kinesthetic* person.

Many people have a combination of two or even all three of these memories. (And if you *smelled* the pine boughs or *tasted* the candy canes, you're not odd. Olfactory and gustatory ways of processing information are certainly legitimate, but if these are your primary styles of processing information, you're in the minority.)

Use this exercise to help you determine the type of entrance meditation that will best fit your purposes. If you're a visual person, you might enjoy a brief guided imagery. Close your eyes and picture your current situation (relationship, day, problem, whatever) in your imagination. Follow the images wherever they lead you. After a few minutes, open your eyes and begin to write.

If you're an auditory person, try journaling with your favorite music in the background. Close your eyes and let the music take you to a place you find relaxing, safe, and secure.

If you're a kinesthetic person, take a hot bath. Do some yoga stretches. Jog in place. Close your eyes and take note of your internal feelings. Relax.

If you're olfactory, burn incense or light a scented candle. If you're gustatory, pour a cup of tea or have munchies handy.

If you're a combination, you can really have fun. You can pick and choose as the mood strikes. You can experiment and find out what works best. You'll find, over time, that your entrance meditations may change depending on your mood, the time of day you're journaling, what you want to accomplish in a journaling session, and which technique you plan to use.

Whatever else you do, and if you don't do anything else, *breathe*. Deep breathing changes your whole metabolism and is the most centering, grounding, relaxing thing you can do for yourself. Breath is a celebration of life. Five good, deep, slow inhales and exhales will take about a minute and will do wonders for your concentration and focus. If you don't believe it, try it.

Suggested entrance meditations are included at the end of some technique chapters. Try them out. Read them into a tape recorder. Adapt them so that they fit your special circumstances. Or make up some of your own.

TWO: DATE EVERY ENTRY

If you only develop one habit in your journal, let it be this one. Dating every entry allows for the emergence of the cycles, patterns, and trends discussed earlier. It also allows you to chronologically reconstruct your journal by date, should you choose to file your journal entries in a loose-leaf binder.

Even if you use a bound book, dating every entry is an excellent habit to develop. Your burning issue of today may seem like something that deserves a permanent place in your memory bank, but chances are pretty good that a year or two from now, you won't be able to pinpoint its exact moment in time.

There is also the factor of the "negative space." In *The New Diary,* Tristine Rainer states: "As it is in poetry, silence is a part of the form. The blank time between entries speaks of great activity, or deserts of experiences, or absence for other reasons. The silence in diaries can speak as eloquently as words."

Several years ago, when I was in a painful marriage, I wrote a long, heartrending, cathartic entry about my difficulties. I posed the ever-present question of leaving the marriage, chewed on it a while, and didn't come up with any resolution. Months passed. The next time I picked up my journal, it was with the intention of again letting off steam about the situation, which hadn't improved a bit. But when I reread my prior entry and realized that I had made absolutely no progress in resolving my situation, I wrote instead about seeking counseling. My internal debate resulted in my first appointment with a supportive and sensitive therapist.

THREE: KEEP WHAT YOU WRITE

Even the most maudlin, the most inane, the most abstract journal entries can contain seeds for future insight; the tapestry of your life will be woven with the weaker entries punctuating the stronger. Unfinished lists, a letter that started out all wrong, a paragraph that ends midphrase can all relay significant information about your personal process.

When you learn to read between, below, above, and through the lines in your journal, you develop an attitude of expectancy, and you'll be richly rewarded. Part of this attitude of expectancy is to trust your process, wherever it may lead you. You can always go back and edit out the entries that clutter your journal. But for starters, get into the habit of filing every last scrap of paper you write on. (The backs of envelopes, cocktail napkins, and other journal miscellany can be taped or stapled to a regular piece of paper for easy storage.)

FOUR: WRITE QUICKLY, AND DON'T WORRY ABOUT YOUR PENMANSHIP

Writing quickly increases spontaneity and removes mental blinders. It also serves as an effective antidote to dreaded "writer's block."

The motor activity of writing quickly engages your "left brain" (the part of your intellectual process that is analytical, rational, discerning and which makes judgments) and thus frees up your "right brain" (the part of your process that is free, fluid, creative, and imaginative) to sneak in the back door. And when you write quickly, you aren't as likely to consciously think about what you're writing. The net result: you'll tap into intuitive and subconscious information much more readily. As a bonus, you can get more journal writing done in less time when you put pen to paper and don't come up for air!

Many people say, "But what about legibility? When I write quickly, I scribble and no one can read it!" The question is, can *you* read it? In your journal, you're the only one for whom it must be decipherable!

And speaking of handwriting, it's a good idea to allow your penmanship to be however it wants to be, anytime you're writing in your journal. There will be times when you're feeling free and flowing. Let your handwriting reflect that. And there will be times when you're feeling tight and cramped. Your writing can mirror that, as well.

Your handwriting can be an amazing barometer of your inner process, but you can also use it to help you achieve desired results. If you're feeling like there's too much structure in your life, try writing on blank paper, or in circles, or diagonally across the page. If you're feeling mired in confusion, try printing very legibly. If you're feeling overburdened and hopelessly adult and responsible, make the sticks-and-circles letters of a first-grader. Christina Baldwin, in *One to One: Self-Understanding Through Journal Writing*, explains it this way:

> If I ever got scared of writing I'd go right back to that first-grade level and play with it again. I'd buy some big-lined sheets of school paper and a fat pencil and start writing the alphabet over and over again. Using again these tools of my early years puts me in touch with the excitement they held for me at age six. I even write with

my tongue sticking out. . . . Then I'd go out and buy myself a set of those plastic magnetic alphabets and make big, unpronounceable words on my refrigerator door. I won't worry anymore about spelling. I won't worry anymore about "full and complete" sentences. I won't worry what anybody is going to think—I will just write for the fun of it.

FIVE: START WRITING, KEEP WRITING

Nothing will shut down your journaling process faster than sitting before a blank page, cogitating and ruminating over what to write, how to write it, whether it will sound right, and whether it's exactly what you want to say. It's akin to going to the swimming pool with the intention of having a hard workout, and standing at the side of the pool for 30 minutes, wondering if the water is too cold, if you'll get chlorine in your eyes, or if you'll have time to dry your hair before your next appointment. Just jump in!

Begin anywhere:

- with the date
- with a Springboard (see chapter 7)
- with your predominant mood or feeling
- with a question
- with the ending
- with the Best Thing
- with the Worst Thing

Just begin. Trust that it doesn't matter where you begin; if you'll only get started, your intuitive sense will lead you where you really want to be.

You might want to start with a Time Capsule (see chapter 15) of your day:

I closed my first sale today! Felt strong and powerful in the meeting, and it went off without a hitch. I was very proud of myself. Afterward, Carol and Jim took me out to lunch to celebrate. I felt, for the first time, that I was part of the team. . . .

Or you could start with a List (see chapter 10):

Things I Absolutely, Positively, Irrevocably Must Do [or Cancel, or Delegate] Today

Or you could start with the immediate moment:

Same place, same time. Old yellow leaves fall from the maple outside my blinds. Candle, music, gray sky. This is the same place I have ever been. This is the place that follows me around.

More often than not, wherever you start will lead you where you need and want to be. In the first example, Wanda went on to describe to herself the frustrations she felt being the "new kid on the block" at work. In the second example, Chloe ended up with 10 "must-do's" for the day, each accompanied by a satisfying check mark and a follow-up entry about lightening up on her jam-packed schedule. And Stephen's melancholy mood led him into reflections on a former love:

What came after that . . . was never more than dead nostalgia. We replayed the old tapes and shoved them in each other's faces to cover our disappointment and to hide from our own loss. We never should have done that, Jenna. I wish we had rolled up that futon, tossed the empty bottle of cabernet in the recycling bin, and never looked back.

Once you get started, keep going. It's awfully tempting to allow distractions in, to remember the phone call you absolutely must make, to write one paragraph, reread it seven times, and search for the precise verb that will capture the essence of the action. Keep going. Remember to write quickly. Just let it flow.

If you find yourself absolutely stuck and can't seem to get the knack of allowing the writing process to continue, try focusing your attention on the tip of your pen. Just watch the words flow out of your pen, notice how you intuitively know how to form the letters, how your hand returns automatically to the left side of the page when you reach the end of the line. This will help center you in the present moment, and "nowness" is one of the keys to satisfying journal writing.

Every now and then, you'll goof. You'll write a word or a phrase that's out of context, that isn't really what you meant to say at all. Or you'll leave a letter out of a word, and the omission will create a completely different word. *Keep writing!* Leave these glitches alone! Your little "Freudian slips," in many cases, are your subconscious mind's way of feeding you information.

Now, sometimes a mistake is just a mistake. (After all, Freud himself said that sometimes a cigar is just a cigar!) My rule of thumb is this: the subconscious significance of the glitch is directly proportional to the intensity with which you want to immediately correct it. If you suddenly realize your error and say to yourself in horror, "Wherever did *that* come from?" *leave it alone.* Circle it, write a note in the margin, write the word you *meant* to write above it in parentheses, but allow it to speak to you. Assume that your subconscious mind wanted to get your attention.

Josie, angry with her mother's nonassertiveness in a family situation, noticed that she was acting in a similar way in her own relationship. "Am I turning into my mother?" she asked herself in her journal, except "turning" ended up as "tuning." The resulting question, "Am I *tuning* into my mother?" gave her a very direct message that perhaps the way out of her own situation was to focus on being more compassionate and understanding with her parents.

Judith debated the pros and cons of a decision. "I can feel the internal dialogue beginning," she meant to say, but instead wrote, "I can feel the internal *deluge* beginning." Suddenly it became clear to her that her paralysis in the decision-making process resulted from the avalanche of information that was knocking her off her feet.

Your subconscious is so clever that it doesn't even need words to give you clues to your inner process. Patricia was in a wheelchair after an automobile accident that could potentially have crippled her permanently. After a Guided Imagery exercise, she and her classmates drew pictures of the various stages of their inner journeys. Much to the delight of the entire class, Patricia "forgot" to draw herself in the wheelchair by the third picture! (As a P.S., within three months Patricia had abandoned her wheelchair in favor of a walker!)

SIX: TELL THE COMPLETE TRUTH FASTER

This phrase, which I have borrowed from author, rebirther, and seminar leader Sondra Ray, sums up the essence of journal writing: Go to the bottom line. You'll get the best results if you don't try to "snooker" yourself.

Let's say that you have this crazy urge to bag the spouse and kids, grab the dog, jump in the van, and go live in a tepee in Montana for six months. This is one way to approach this scenario in your journal:

> I don't know why I'm feeling *this way* [what way are you feeling?]. I *don't like* these feelings very much [why? because they're scary? foreign? unsettling?]. I guess what I

really need is exercise to *work myself through this* [what are you working through?]. I think I'll go mow the lawn.

And here's another, perhaps more helpful, approach:

Seems like for the last few weeks I've been preoccupied with escaping from it all. I've got this crazy yen to get far, far away from the daily grind. It's a frightening feeling because it calls into question all that I think I hold dear. Would I really trade my family for the company of the dog and an extended period of solitude? Sometimes it feels like it. . . .

I first started noticing these feelings about a month ago, when it all started coming down on me at once. Quarterly reports at work. The annual fund-raising drive at church. The kids need entire new wardrobes for school. Time and money. Money and time. I can't have one if I'm going to have the other, but it seems like I really can't have either.

Now we're getting somewhere. It isn't about wanting to run away from home after all. That's just the symptom.

It's perfectly natural to feel some reluctance and hesitation while you are getting acquainted with this new approach to self-awareness. Your relationship with your journal is just like any other relationship in your life, and you can look to your other relationships for clues on how to best formulate your journal friendship.

Any new relationship needs time to build trust, develop confidence, establish rapport. If you're a person who forms friendships easily, you're likely to throw yourself enthusiastically into your journal from the start. If you prefer to maintain reserve and get to know another person gradually over time, then allow yourself to develop the trust in your journal at a pace that feels comfortable and right for you. You'll know what feels right by the level of satisfaction and enjoyment you're deriving.

What about the uglies? What about the times you're so furious you could pop? What about the black fantasies? What about the stuff that's really *bad?*

Get it out of your system! Your journal is a perfectly appropriate place to express yourself—*all* of yourself. Tell the complete truth faster. Fifteen minutes of ventilating on paper can save you a migraine headache. If it's too awful to even reread, much less keep, you can suspend the "keep what you write" suggestion and indulge yourself in the wonderful act of ripping it up and stomping on it. Or flushing it down the toilet. Or burning it in the fireplace. Make a ritual out of it!

Sports enthusiasts swear by the virtue of exercise as a stress reducer. Journal writing can be a fine adjunct. When you move your negative emotions *out* of your body through exercise or writing, they aren't lurking around to cause tension or disease via tight muscles, stiff necks, headaches, ulcers, or heart attacks.

You are entitled to *all* of your feelings. Anger is not a mistake. Neither is fear or grief. They are pure, honest, human emotions. It's what you do with them that makes them productive or destructive. Acknowledging them and dealing with them constructively are the first steps in converting the energy to something healthy and positive.

SEVEN: PROTECT YOUR OWN PRIVACY

Probably the most universal concern about journal writing is the fear that somebody (spouse, child, parent, boss, friend, stranger) will read the journal without your permission.

It's a legitimate concern. If you feel like there's someone reading over your shoulder, it's difficult to keep what you write, to start writing and keep writing, and to tell the complete truth faster.

The journal, by definition, is a private book. It is a collection of innermost thoughts and feelings; it is uniquely *you*. To have someone read your journal is literally to have someone read your mind, and also your heart and soul.

Get in the habit of protecting your own privacy.

Ultimately, the responsibility for privacy remains with each individual who is writing a journal. And getting in the habit of protecting your own privacy is very good practice for getting in the habit of taking responsibility for other areas of your life.

You can protect your own privacy in many different ways. First of all, find a storage place for your journal between uses so that it will not be a temptation for others in your household. During my troubled marriage, I used my journal extensively to process my rage, pain, and feelings of futility. So I kept my journal in my briefcase. It was always with me. And whoever snoops around in somebody else's briefcase? I didn't tell anyone where it was, of course. I just discreetly filed it away after each use.

Cecelia keeps her journal in the laundry room, right there with the detergent and the fabric softener. She uses the 30-minute wash cycle as her own private time. "I never knew laundry could be so rewarding!" she says with a laugh. Kevin, a real estate salesman who insists that he "lives in his car," has developed the habit of storing his journal under the front seat. It's never further away than a quick walk out the door.

Find a place for your journal. It can be kept in your nightstand, your dresser drawer, a file cabinet, a bookshelf. Depending on the level of discretion necessary in your household, it can be an openly acknowledged storage place or somewhere all your own. During particularly stressful times of your life, you may want to entrust certain journal entries to a valued friend. Or get in the habit of carrying your journal with you. You'll enjoy the comfort of knowing you can write whenever you want, wherever you are.

Many times you can protect your own privacy simply by making a calm, clear, reasonable statement to other members of your household. "I'm starting a journal of my thoughts and feelings," you might say to your spouse, roommate, parents, children. "I'll keep my journal in its own special place, and I would appreciate it if you would respect my privacy by not reading it without my permission. Will you agree to do that?"

Protect your privacy in other ways, as well. Reserve the first page of a new journal for your name, address, phone number, and a brief statement:

> This is my private journal. If you should find it, I would very much appreciate its return. Please obtain my permission first if you wish to read it. Should I decline, I hope that you will not be offended.

Or you can be even more direct:

> Contains information of no use or interest to anyone except the owner. Please return if found. Thank you for respecting my privacy.

My journal for a month-long trip to England carried this message:

> This notebook contains a journal of my stay in your beautiful country. Should I lose it in my travels, I would be very grateful if you would mail it to me at the address shown. Thank you very much!

I taped the appropriate amount of British postage to the inside front cover. It was a cheap insurance policy, and I gave the stamps to my niece upon my journal's safe return home.

EIGHT: WRITE NATURALLY

If there is one inviolate rule of journal writing, it is that there simply are no rules. Writing naturally means that you do what works for you and that you don't worry about what you're not doing in the journal.

Geri attended a Write On! workshop and fell in love with the possibilities of her journal. She filled up one entire spiral notebook writing Character Sketches (see chapter 8) one right after another. She wrote Character Sketches about every member of her family, every friend she'd ever had, every person that she worked with. When she ran out of Character Sketches to write, she wrote them of famous people and of people she hadn't met yet but wanted to. She wrote Character Sketches until she had exhausted herself of Character Sketches, and then she moved on to Clustering (see chapter 9). She clustered her thoughts, her feelings, her PMS, her business activities, her friends, her moods, her to-do list, her daughter's birthday party—you name it. When Clustering lost its appeal, she moved on to her dreams (see chapter 19). And so on. *That's* writing naturally!

Writing naturally means that you pick up your journal when the mood strikes and put it down when the mood shifts. It means that you allow for changes in focus, in technique, in penmanship, in point of view. It means that an Unsent Letter (see chapter 17) can evolve into a Dialogue (see chapter 11), or that a List of 100 (see chapter 12) may only have one item on it. It means that you may write a hundred pages in a weekend and then not look at your journal for a month.

I went through a stage in high school when I would only write with a purple Lindy stick pen in a Big Chief tablet. (To this day, a purple Lindy pen or a Big Chief tablet will instantly put me in the mood to journal!) Writing naturally means you indulge in your idiosyncracies, otherwise known as Life's Small Pleasures.

Writing naturally means that you make it up as you go along.

Writing naturally means that you trust your inner wisdom to guide you to the places you need to go.

Writing naturally means that you freely create your diary world with confidence and ease.

Writing naturally means that you give yourself permission to play. And to cry. And to cuss. And to celebrate. And to be fully, vibrantly alive.

Writing naturally means that you allow yourself to use your journal as a blank canvas onto which the rich and intricate portrait of your life can be painted as it organically emerges.

There is only one person who can write the story of your life, with all its foibles, follies, treasures, and tears. That person is you.

Writing naturally means that you let yourself be you.

4

CHOICES

Choices! There are lots of them. Blank paper or lined? Fountain pen or number 2 pencil? Steno pad or blank bound book? One journal or several? How do you find something you wrote two years ago? Do you write every day? Morning or evening? For how long? The choices can get downright complex! Let's take them one at a time.

Remember this: you can change your mind whenever you want to! If something you try doesn't work for you, try something else.

THE BOOK

Among your many choices are:

• **Blank bound books.** Stationery stores and bookstores carry lovely blank bound books, some with lined pages, some without. A collection of these journals makes an attractive display on a bookshelf, and they are easy to carry with you. Most blank books are in the $6 to $12 range, which makes them a nice gift to ask for or give. The two primary disadvantages: some people are intimidated or inhibited by the permanence of the pages, and it is difficult to write close to either inside margin without cracking the book's spine.

• **Spiral notebooks.** My personal favorite, spiral notebooks are available virtually everywhere. They're inexpensive and come in a rainbow of cover colors and designs. I buy them by the dozen. You may keep the notebooks intact or tear out the pages to file in a three-ring binder. If you choose the latter, buy prepunched notebooks with perforated pages to avoid confetti-bunching under the binder rings. The primary disadvantages of spiral notebooks are: 1) they're not very elegant; 2) some left-handers have a problem with the spiral (Ampad makes a "Left-Write" notebook); 3) spiral notebooks with blank pages aren't as readily available. Otherwise, I can't find a thing wrong with them.

• **Three-ring binders.** These are also inexpensive and can be filled with lined or blank paper. Some journalers don't like three-ring notebooks because they're too reminiscent of school days. Smaller notebooks can be tossed in a tote bag or briefcase; larger ones are bulky to carry around. Buy notebooks with inside pockets for storage of journal miscellany. Also invest in a three-hole punch.

• **Artist's oversized sketch pads.** You can use these like scrapbooks, mounting in the punctuation marks of your days (fortune-cookie fortunes, "Cathy" cartoons, ticket stubs, birthday cards). If you're artistically inclined, you'll enjoy the extra room to doodle or paint. Buy ones with spiral bindings so the pages don't fall out.

• **Scraps of paper, backs of envelopes, cocktail napkins.** These can be tossed into a shoebox or mounted and filed in a three-ring notebook. Try to remember to date your entries!

WRITING INSTRUMENTS

Whatever you use, make sure it feels good:

• **Pencils.** A number 4 (hard) lead has a completely different feel from a number 2 (soft), so before you rule out pencils entirely, experiment. If you're devoted to wooden pencils, invest in a wall-mounted hand-crank sharpener or a medium-grade battery-operated desk model. (The cheaper desk models tend to eat the pencil rather than sharpen it.) Mechanical pencils are fairly inexpensive and come in a variety of grips and weights. If you like pencils, you probably also like to erase, so have several good erasers on hand.

• **Colored pencils.** These are great to illustrate your journal when you're in the mood for a little perking up. Treat yourself to some "real" ones from an art supply store.

• **Pens.** A thousand choices, but one criterion: make sure it feels good! The ink in some cheap pens has an unpleasant, sour odor. That smell alone is enough to make me toss a pen in the trash. I also pitch any pen that smudges dollops of ink all over the page. Cross and Waterman pens, of course, are to die for, and the price reflects it. Don't *ever* loan them! Not to worry: there are many inexpensive pens that have a clean, firm write. When you find a brand you like, buy a box of your favorite color and several each of other colors. Try a fountain pen! (They come with ink cartridges in several pretty colors.)

• **Colored pens.** Buy a set of 24 or 30 colored ballpoint pens. You may have to go to a "five-and-dime" to find them. Generally speaking, they're not very good writing pens, but it's fun to have a wide variety of colors. You can also find a wide variety of colored felt-tip pens in art supply stores.

• **Highlighter pens.** The neon-colored, transparent highlighter pens are handy for cross-referencing or noting action steps to take.

BEGINNING A NEW JOURNAL

Sarah has developed a ritual for beginning her journal volumes. (She uses the three-ring binder format, currently with blank paper.) First, she selects a notebook color. Her selection is often influenced by whatever process she is currently undergoing, but she swears that even when she picks a color because she likes it, the color becomes metaphoric. Next, she writes a greeting to the new journal to open the communication. Her current volume, a black notebook, opens with:

Greetings, journal of my journey into my deepest depths:

It feels good to be where I am and at the place where I am ready and able to welcome you into my life. I have taken a giant leap in the past week. I am now in a new stage, a deeper level of my process of unfoldment and self-realization. . . . Thank you for being with me and providing me the sanctuary that only a journal can provide. I am sure we will travel far and deep together, always with the intention of healing into more perfect wholeness. Bless you and bless my process as we explore and travel together.

"From that point on," Sarah said, "the journal takes off and develops its own theme, almost its own personality. Each one is very different, but every one is an ally."

Sarah also uses the beginning of a new journal volume to check in with herself about her choices. If she's been writing on blank paper, she asks herself if it would feel good to have lines. The volume completed before her black journal (the yellow journal, the journal of joy and light) had many entries in green ink. "I knew in the first entry of the black journal that the green pen wasn't right," she said. "The black journal seems to want black and red ink."

In short, Sarah *honors* her journal. Her journal is an ongoing, valued part of her life. She takes the time and energy to develop a relationship with her journal. And that is another way of saying that she takes the time and energy to develop a relationship with herself.

SMORGASBORD OR A LA CARTE?

Dr. Ira Progoff, one of the first psychologists to study and work with the personal process journal as a therapeutic tool, created a seminar called the Intensive Journal Workshop™ in 1966. (The text and guide for this seminar is called *At a Journal Workshop*.) One of the hallmarks of the Intensive Journal™

method is the three-ring notebook issued to each student at registration. The notebook is divided into 21 sections, such as Period Log; Daily Log; Dialogue Dimension; Imagery Extensions; Now: The Open Moment. This is one method of "à la carte" journal writing: grouping your entries together with others of their kind.

I've known journal writers who use several different notebooks for different areas of their lives—a green one for money, a yellow one for upbeat topics, a red one for career, a blue one for relationships. This is another "à la carte" method.

"A la carte" approaches are like a zoom lens on a camera. You must stand back a good distance to see the whole picture, but you can get great close-up shots. It's difficult to see how an individual entry fits into the larger context of your life. But you can track with great accuracy one segment of your life. A cross-referencing system is helpful for "à la carte" journals.

I am basically a "smorgasbord" journal writer. I like to take a little bit of everything and put it all on the same plate. Therefore, you'll find my things-to-do-today list nestled up against last night's dream, and I'm likely to color a picture on the flip side of a project outline. In this way the various aspects of my life, like twins *in utero*, learn to share the space and co-exist cooperatively; they nudge to the foreground as they individually need more nourishment and attention.

"Smorgasbord" journals are like a wide-angled lens. You can get close to a 360-degree view, but you have to look pretty hard to find the details. Some sort of an indexing system is very useful.

There may be times when it is appropriate to separate out parts of your journal. If you're going through a divorce, there could be several reasons for keeping a separate divorce journal. You might want to chronicle the undiluted process so that you can remember what it was like to go through a divorce. You may want to have everything you've written about the divorce in one place so you can be sure it's with you at all times. Or you may want to create a ritual in which you burn the divorce journal when it's time to get on with your life.

When I am in dream therapy, I honor the therapeutic process by giving my dreams a pretty book all their own.

HOW MUCH IS TOO MUCH?

I once had a lover break up with me by leaving a good-bye letter and roses that must have cost $50 on my dining room table at midnight. Fortunately, there was a long weekend ahead for which I didn't have plans (except with *him*), so I stayed up all night crying buckets of tears and writing wrathful Unsent Letters. When the grocery store opened the next morning, I ventured out only long enough to buy three pounds of boiled shrimp and one pound of Oreos. Then I came home, closed all my curtains, locked all my doors, put a new message on the answering machine ("I'm having a broken heart. Please call back on Sunday"), and journaled nonstop for 72 hours. For three solid days I did nothing but cry, eat shrimp and Oreos, listen to sad music ("Desperado" by the Eagles was my favorite), and write in my journal. Oh yes, and smell those $50 roses.

By Sunday afternoon I was bored out of my mind. I was bored with journaling, I was bored with "Desperado," I was bored with shrimp and Oreos, and I was most definitely bored with the man who had left me! I was even bored with the roses.

It was my "personal best" for recovery from a broken heart. Three days, start to finish! Oh sure, I was a little raw for a couple of months. But it wasn't anything like my broken hearts of yore. I'm absolutely convinced that it was the act of total immersion into the pain—and having the journal there to guide and direct the process—that allowed me to move into the misery, through it, and out the other side.

CHOICES

I tell this story in my classes because the question always arises: can there be too much of a good thing?

Of course. Anything done to excess, including something as healthy as journal writing (or exercise or meditation or carrot juice), can be destructive. That is because when you are overemphasizing one thing, even a healthy one, you are underemphasizing something else. So be aware of striving for balance. Jim Rohn, the popular motivational speaker, says, "There are two things to avoid with your journal. One is never writing in it; the other is always writing in it. In the first case, you participate in life without observing it. In the second case, you observe life without participating in it."

There are times, however—like my lost weekend—when it is perfectly appropriate to cloister yourself away and do very little else but write. A student in a recent class consistently wrote 75 to 100 pages per week in her journal. Not coincidentally, she worked herself through a major life decision that involved moving to the East Coast. I spoke with her just before she moved, and she told me that after the class ended, she took a two-month vacation from her journal. She thought she'd probably be starting up again soon. Balance.

On the other hand, how much is enough? If there's a question about journal writing that has no one answer, this is it.

Personally, my minimum maintenance level is to write at least three times a week for at least 30 minutes at a time, and this is what I request of my students. (I often write much more than this; my journaling seems to go in cycles.) If my writing falls beneath this minimum, I become aware that certain areas of my life aren't going as well as they could. Communication with my partner might break down, or I don't sleep well, or I feel foggy, aimless, or ungrounded. These are all signals that I'm not taking care of myself. My favorite antidote is to disappear for 30 minutes or an hour with my journal.

But try not to get too caught up in the details of "how often" and "for how long" and "how much." Don't confuse the *activity* of journal writing with the *purpose* of journal writing. You're not doing this to meet a quota, win a prize, fulfill someone else's expectations, or be the "perfect" journal writer. So how often do you want to write? And for how long? And how much? That's the proper combination for you. Don't feel that you're being selfish because you want to take time for yourself. Who else is going to give it to you if you don't?

PRIVACY

Another question that frequently comes up: "Should I share my journal with my lover, husband, sister, mother, child?" Do you *want* to? If not, then by all means, don't. If you do, then I recommend you check it out with your would-be audience. Some people are not comfortable with another's intimate thoughts and feelings. Ask permission before you share.

And of course you wouldn't *dream* of reading someone else's journal without their express invitation, would you?

Well, maybe you would. Perhaps the most lucid discussion of this temptation comes from Kay Leigh Hagan's *Internal Affairs:*

> For everyone who ever wanted to read another's journal or succumbed to that temptation, I want you to know you are not alone. . . . At difficult points [in relationships], reading someone's journal seems infinitely easier than discussing insecurities face to face. I am not condoning this attitude; I am simply acknowledging a probability. . . . Writing your personal thoughts, observations, dreams, fears, and opinions in your private journal is not and can never be wrong. But reading another's private writings without permission is an act of violation and betrayal.

CROSS-REFERENCING AND INDEXING

Just as the *act* of journal writing allows you to move fluidly within the present moment, the *art* of journal writing allows you to move fluidly within the overall context of your life, as recorded in your journals. Ideally, then, the art of journal writing includes an orderly system of journal management.

If you want to be able to find specific journal entries without poring over old volumes (a wonderful way to spend an afternoon, by the way), you can develop some sort of a cross-reference or indexing system.

The journal you receive when you take a Progoff workshop is broken into sections with color coded dividers, each printed with its section's name. When I am using my Progoff journal, I cross-reference the sections by color-coding entries with transparent highlighter pens.

The Depth Dimension section of the Progoff journal, for instance, is blue. The Depth Dimension includes dreams, dream enlargements, and imageries. When I work in the yellow section (Daily Log) and something in my *outer* life is matching something in my *inner* life as evidenced by a dream recorded in the blue section, I highlight the pertinent Daily Log passages in blue, alerting me to look for a related dream in the Depth Dimension. Likewise, I highlight the dream in yellow, telling me that this dream is explained in the Daily Log.

There are other ways to cross-reference, of course, but this is the easiest way I have found. Eventually my Progoff notebook is filled. When it's time to clean it out, I merge the different sections together by date and house them in a separate three-ring binder.

If you're taking a "smorgasbord" approach, a written index kept by date is probably the simplest way to keep track of major issues. Let's say that you're exploring a new relationship and thinking about quitting your job. At any point, it might be helpful to pull together all of the entries on either theme and read them within the context of each other.

Keep a page in the back of your journal for each major theme. When your journal entry includes information about the theme, make a note of the date and a one-line summary on the index page.

Many people never index or cross-reference their journals. Should you decide to, beware of the tendency to get compulsive. The best rule of thumb: use indexes and cross-references only when it enhances your journal process.

MOVING ON

Sooner or later, every journal ends. It will be time to move on to another book of your life.

By the way, this may or may not correspond with the actual completion of a book or notebook. If you feel an internal shift happening—a new chapter of your life beginning—by all means give yourself permission to end a journal volume (even if it's not finished!) and begin a new one.

Sarah ends her journals with a completion letter summing up the themes that emerged for her:

Well, journal of discovery and joy. . . .

I must have known that our time together was drawing near its end. I have so enjoyed our four months together— they have been filled with journeys to places I didn't even know existed.

I have discovered with you an inner, infinite well of joy, beauty, love, creativity, expression, courage, strength, power, depth, love, compassion, wisdom, happiness. You have been a constant source of believing in myself, pushing a little further, stretching and loving. I am sure I will visit you often. You have helped me to feel inner freedom for the first time since I can remember. This inner freedom allows me to move on to the next level, the level of my deepest depths. I could not have done it without you.

As you end your journal volume, give it a title which represents the themes represented. (Sometimes you'll want to name your journal at the beginning, as Heidi did: "This is my third journal. Honesty is its name because that's what I want to work on next. . . .") This is also a good time to review your journal in its entirety. Be sure to put the dates of its first and last entries on the cover or title page so that you can easily locate a given time frame in your life.

The choices can indeed be many, but so can the rewards. Allow your journal choices to be a statement about your willingness to nurture yourself. Experiment until you find your own right combinations. But above all else . . . do what works for *you!*

5

JOURNALS TO GO: 19 WAYS TO WRITE FOR UNDER 15 MINUTES EACH

> **"I gave up chocolate. I gave up expresso.
> I gave up the Count (that naughty man) and his little
> house in Cap Ferrat. This Waterman pen, however, is not
> negotiable. I must have something thrilling with which
> to record my boredom."**
>
> **—Waterman Pen Company advertisement**

Ah yes, the boredom. It's easy enough to find time for melancholy introspection when there's nothing else to do. But what about those languid nights of chocolate, conversation, and expresso? What about the times when that scoundrel, the Count, is whisking you off to Cap Ferrat yet again? What about those times when you don't have enough time to *live* your life, much less *record* it?

Don't worry. You can keep up your journal in under fifteen minutes a day without ever feeling bored or boring. Here's how:

1. Keep a one-year diary. They come in an attractive assortment of cover designs; many have matching scrapbooks and photo albums. Because the format restricts you to around a hundred words, writing takes 10 minutes or less a day. And keeping your one-year diary on the nightstand by your bed has a sort of Victorian simplicity that is madly appealing.

2. In the evening, write one adjective describing your day on your wall calendar. Then, underneath it, write one adjective describing how you want tomorrow to be. This takes about one minute and becomes a fascinating exercise in creating your own reality.

3. Best Thing/Worst Thing Springboards are great for the one-year diary. Repeated use of these Springboards will give you a running commentary on the highlights and blackouts of your life.

4. Pick a theme word for a week or a month—happiness, loneliness, confusion, clarity, anger, passion, change, etc. Spend 5 to 15 minutes each day writing about how you experienced the theme word that day.

5. Find a moment from your day to capture in poetry or prose—the rainbow out your office window, the elation when the home team won the game, the luxury of a bubble bath. If you can't find a moment to record, slow down a little. And start expecting miracles. They might just show up.

6. Set the kitchen timer for 15 minutes. Quit writing when it dings.

7. Write a description of a stranger—the person across from you on the bus, the little blond kid in the bright red dress, someone you'll never see again, someone you haven't met yet.

8. Jot down the one-liners of philosophy, absurdity, or spiritual revelation that wander through your mind. Hugh Prather's *Notes to Myself* is a collection of such "random" thoughts.

9. Write a list of "10 Things I Want Off My List by Tomorrow." Keep this list with you throughout the day. Cross off items as you finish them.

10. Write a Win List of anything at all that went right during the day. (Yes, there are days when "getting out of bed" counts.) If you are in recovery from any sort of addictive behavior, be sure to list your recovery *every single day* as a win. Bob Trask of the ARAS Foundation says he strives to list at least 37 individual wins each day. And again, if you're not having many wins, invite them into your life. Expect a miracle.

11. Record a fantasy. Close your eyes and think about what it would be like if your job, relationship, children, or sex life were perfect. Then write about your inner journey.

12. Write your journal on three-by-five index cards. File entries by subject or date in a recipe box.

13. Write a Memorandum of the Day in your business appointment book.

14. Write a postcard. Send it to yourself. (Here's the ultimate travel tip for journal writers on the go—write your daily log on the back of picture postcards!)

15. Draw a picture of your present moment with pencil, crayons, oil pastels, charcoal, water colors, markers, finger paints, ballpoint pen. Give it a name. Write about it if you want to and have time.

16. "Flow-write" for 10 to 15 minutes. Start anywhere, go where you please.

17. Thumb through an old magazine until a picture "sings" to you. Clip the picture and paste it in your journal. Write about it.

18. Doodle a cartoon. Joan has elevated cartooning to its own journal form. "A line here, a circle there, a stick man, a silly face. . . . Anyone can doodle successfully!" Joan claims. "Cartoons let me look at the lighter side of a situation. The cartoon reproduced here humorously captures my frustration

with weekly mountain hikes planned by my enthusiastic husband."

19. Write a prayer. Write a letter to God, your Higher Self, Jesus Christ, your guardian angel, your patron saint, your inner guide. Let these entities write a letter to you. Try this for 30 days. You'll be glad you did.

Nature loves balance, and so there will be plenty of languid times to even out the hectic spans. These quieter times are the moments when you will drink deeply from the journal well. But your time crunch doesn't mean you must sacrifice your journal, and your journal doesn't mean you must sacrifice your time. As it is with nature, there is balance where you seek it.

6
FOR MEN ONLY

Dear Bruce Springsteen,
Me again. I'm getting off on this. I never thought I'd
have this much to talk about. . . . It's getting to be
almost like a diary.

—Kevin Majors
Dear Bruce Springsteen

In the novel *Dear Bruce Springsteen*, 14-year-old Terry Blanchard writes letters to his hero. And in the process of examining the contents of his heart, Terry comes to a dawning awareness that he's a pretty neat kid.

Although the personal process journal is popularly thought of as a women's instrument for reflection and self-discovery, there are plenty of men writing in plenty of notebooks. Here, four of them share with you what it's like to be a man and write a journal.

ROBERT

[Robert, 41, has worked as a railroad switchman for 14 years. He is completing a master's degree in Jungian psychology. His interests include astrology, organic gardening, downhill skiing, and sports of all kinds.]

Journaling is for girls. At least, that's what many men think. That's what I thought until a few years ago. Now I've changed my mind.

I don't write in a journal on any consistent basis. I don't deal with my feelings with any consistency, either. But I am learning to do both, because they feed upon one another. The more that I take responsibility for my emotional side, the more I want and need to write down what is happening to me.

I started to use a journal about five years ago to record dreams. I found that writing helped with understanding the whole dream process. As a graduate student in psychology, I was required to keep a journal for many of my classes, so I became more used to it as time went on.

One of my favorite times to write in the journal is while I'm skiing. I keep a small notebook in my jacket pocket and write on the ski lift or while I'm resting. It seems like my thought process is much clearer when I'm skiing. My thoughts and feelings seem to come from a place that is deep within me, and I feel they are very important. I've kept track of a lot of my most creative thinking this way.

I sometimes feel that maybe I don't really write in a journal because I don't do it with any regularity. But then I remember that there are no rules to journaling, so I guess it isn't necessary to feel guilty about it.

My mate and I share a community journal; we both write in

it on an ongoing basis. She gave it to us for Christmas last year. It tends to be somewhat uneven because I write much less than she does, but that's okay with both of us. It's a nice place to tell her some of the things I have a hard time saying out loud.

I've been studying astrology for several years, and I feel I understand my own astrological chart and life at a deeper level when I journal about the core issues that I'm dealing with. One issue that shows up in my chart and also in my relationships is my difficulties with personal power—giving it all away, keeping it all, or sharing it. Journaling helps me to understand where I've come from, where I am now, and where I seem to be headed.

I think that, overall, journaling allows me to tune into parts of myself that otherwise would wither and die from lack of recognition. All the great masters said it was necessary to "know thyself" before any great learning could take place. My journal allows me to know myself at increasingly deeper and deeper levels.

JACK

[Jack is a 29-year-old student, writer, and poet. His interests include T'ai Chi, traveling, and woodworking.]

I first started keeping a journal in 1972. That's also the year I started shutting the door to my room. It was essential to me that my journal be something completely secret and separate, something just for me. I was in seventh or eighth grade. I remember going shopping with my sisters and one of their friends. We split up for an hour or two, going our own directions to shop, then met again by one of those instant photo booths where you could get your picture taken for a quarter.

I had bought a blank steno pad and a new blue pen, and I had them in a bag when we met by the photo booth. My sisters' friend kept bothering me to know what I had in the bag. I told her it was a book. Of course, she wanted to see it, but I wouldn't let her. I didn't know how I would explain the steno pad, and I wasn't ready to tell anyone that I was keeping a journal.

After I got that pad and my new blue pen home, I locked them away in a box and hid the box in my closet. Even then I was something of an inventor, and I can remember lying on my bed trying to invent some way that the locked box could explode or release acid to destroy the journal if someone tried to force their way into the box. I never did come up with anything that seemed workable, so I just hid the box deeper in my closet. I wrote in that pad every day until it was filled, and I have kept a journal in some form ever since.

In 1978 I quit college, having no clue what I was doing there in the first place. I have all sorts of journals from the years that followed. It seems that the times when I have gone through the most internal shifting and changing are the times I have done the most journaling. I was hitchhiking all over the country back then, and so mixed in between the poems and drawings that fill those journals are the names of the cities I traveled through. My journal often had to double as a sign board, with the name of the city I was headed toward written across the full page in bold letters so the passing cars and semis could see it as they blew by—Scranton, Sault Ste. Marie, Montreal, Las Cruces, Anchorage—they're all in there.

When I went back to school in Missoula, Montana, I started hopping freight trains. My journals from those years are small spiral notebooks that smell of creosote. They're full of soot and stories about desperate old freight tramps I met and the nights we spent tending their fires, drinking instant coffee and Thunderbird wine.

Right now I keep two journals at the same time. One I keep on a computer and use mostly for recording and working with dreams. The other is a loose-leaf journal in which I put (besides the more ordinary kind of journal entries) pictures, programs from plays I've seen, sketches of furniture I'm building, drawings of dream characters—anything that is flat, can get a hole punched in it, and relates to the fabric of my life. That's what journaling is about to me, really. Over the last 16 years, my journaling has taken many forms, reflecting the changing fabric of my life. I think of journaling as the art form of a lifetime.

DAVID

[David is a 52-year-old math and physics professor who enjoys motorcycling, camping, and living close to nature.]

At age 52 I have discovered journaling, and it is wonderful!

Before taking a course in journal writing, I had never written for myself. I had done a lot of technical writing professionally, but no "creative" writing since my college years. I knew I wasn't good at writing letters, because I never received any positive feedback for them. (Except once, from my mother.)

In the course I took, we submitted our journal entries each week and received them a week later with supportive and helpful comments. At first, I wasn't comfortable having someone else share my innermost thoughts on a regular basis. But the positive feedback I received soon made it okay.

From the first, my major objective was to get in touch with and integrate my subconscious and unconscious minds. My tendency is to stay in control of my feelings and my life by ignoring some of my inner conflicts and compulsions.

During the course, we experimented with all of the different journal-writing techniques you'll find in this book. Some of these were quite useful for me, particularly dialoguing with all the various voices inside of me. I have talked to my inner child, my Higher Self, and the "blocker" who tries to keep me from being successful in new enterprises.

The technique that I have the most fun with, however, is one that I made up myself. It involves writing down a couple of words that simply appear in my mind, then writing without thinking for as long as I can. Sometimes I just write words. Sometimes I describe images. In any case, what comes out is always a surprise and a gift.

After a while, the part of me that needs to remain in control begins to assert itself: "What's going on here?" it says. "Why are we writing this? Where is it leading?" As soon as this happens, my creative burst is over, and nothing more comes.

As I practiced this technique, I realized that the material was coming from my unconscious mind. But what did it mean? The more I practiced, the longer I could sustain the burst, and soon I began to realize that I was writing about myself, and the pieces were meaningful in much the same way that dreams are.

So far, this adaptation of "stream of consciousness" writing has been a wonderful experience. I have written pieces which have shown me where I am in my spiritual development, or have given me insights into my long-ago childhood, or have shown me how I am making my way through the levels of my unconscious mind. But the most important thing, I feel, is simply to *do* it, whether I "analyze" the results or not. Just letting this material flow out of me and become conscious is therapeutic!

ORION

[Orion, 26, is a student of Jungian and transpersonal psychology who is especially interested in the emerging roles of men and masculinity. Here, he shares how he finds in his journal a worthy Blood Brother.]

My Blood Brother is as important to me as life itself. He laughs easily and smiles readily. He's the type people trust instinctively. He's resourceful, courageous, and competent—you can trust him in a time of need. Despite his easy and comfortable way with people, there's a wisdom and aloofness. There's a mystery that lives there that he shares more with me than anyone—but not ever completely with me, either. He listens well; when you have something to say, he concentrates on you, he focuses. You feel supported and loved.

He's got his faults. He's impatient with himself and he gets angry quickly. He's also quick to forgive and forget. He loves nature and sometimes must retreat from the world and even from me to connect with his inner depths. He scares me sometimes, because beneath it all he takes life seriously, very seriously. Usually he can laugh at himself, but he's capable of fits where he can't see perspective. But he always does come back, and I'm there when he does.

He's done more for me than any other person ever could. He is my perspective, for he makes me laugh. When I am at my most depressed, all he needs to do to coax a smile from me is smile himself. He's so absurd, so disrespectful of my self-loathing. He infuriates me, and I need him.

He loves the depth of life; I've never seen anyone with so much compassion. When he talks to me about nature I understand how there are Hindus or mystics who try to avoid killing any life even so small as an ant.

He also loves humor. He can laugh at the worst humor of stand-up comics, the bawdiest, raunchiest, most tasteless stuff and I'll be amazed. When he's funny himself, it's gentle, subtle, often self-deprecating. His ability to laugh at himself rarely deserts him.

Oh, but I've seen him depressed. His eyes go dark and unresponsive; a cloud settles over him and the air goes cold. Where did that serene person go whom I know so well? I've never seen anyone so completely incapacitated. He doesn't cry, nor moan, nor indulge in self-pity; or if he does, he's silent about it. He wraps himself in a cloak of silence and becomes almost catatonic. The strangest thing about these depressions is that though he refuses to speak, he will not remove himself physically from other people. I've seen him in crowded restaurants sitting as though he were alone in the world, oblivious.

When he's like that, his eyes focus on what no one else sees, his hair falling over his forehead, he frightens people. Some say he's psychotic. I know better and am no longer afraid. It's at these times, when I remain a silent presence around him, that I do my service for him. At such times, I know without knowing how I know, that I am somehow his lifeline. My being there allows him to go deeper than he could go otherwise. If I weren't here, I know he would someday go away and never come back. But I am here, and he knows it.

When he does come back, he seldom says anything about where he's been. But he looks at me, his eyes more alive than ever I've seen, filled with compassion and deeply owned pain, and he smiles, a grateful smile, a validating smile, a smile that says more than I think even a poet could say. It says, among so much else: We are Blood Brothers, sworn to closeness, bound by deepest meaning and deepest need. I salute you.

SECTION II

THE JOURNAL TOOLBOX

▼

INTRODUCTION

Think about the toolbox you probably have at home. It has a hammer, a few screwdrivers, some nails, a wrench, a pair of pliers, maybe a drill and some washers.

So when it's time to fix the kitchen sink, you pull out the wrench and a washer. And when a picture needs to be hung, you select the hammer and a nail.

The journal techniques covered in this section are like the tools in the toolbox. Every one is useful in its own way. Some are more appropriate for a particular task than others.

There may be some that don't appeal to you. That's fine.

Personally, I've never been fond of drilling, so I don't use my drill much.

A good toolbox will last you for life, and so will this journal toolbox. Even the techniques that you don't like as well aren't going anywhere. They'll still be here if you want to use them next week, or next month, or next year.

The chapters are self-contained, so don't feel that you must read this section from front to back. Pull out a few tools; try them out. Put them back; try some others.

The examples come from actual journals written by my students, but they are pruned back quite a bit. These edited entries illustrate the "nuts and bolts" of their respective chapter's technique, and they also make powerful reading. All examples, of course, are used with the permission of the writer.

Happy tinkering!

7

SPRINGBOARDS

What should I write about?
—journal workshop and class participants

There will be times when you sit down to write in your journal . . . and nothing will come out. If it's a period of great confusion or activity, there might be a hundred thoughts whirling in your head, each clamoring for attention. If it's a ho-hum day, you may feel as if nothing interesting is going on.

Where to begin?

Jump into the journal waters with a Springboard.

Like the diving board at the swimming pool, a Springboard launches you in a direction. It is the topic sentence of your journal entry. A Springboard helps you focus; it consolidates and clarifies what you want to write about. Like the high dive at the swimming pool, its primary function is to get you into action! So if you start with a Springboard but decide to veer off in a completely different direction as soon as pen hits paper, let it be. The Springboard accomplished its purpose: it got you into the water.

TYPES OF SPRINGBOARDS

There are two basic types of Springboards: statements and questions. As a (very!) general rule, you may find that when you start with a statement, you can more readily access thoughts and facts ("left brain"); beginning with questions tends to generate feelings and explorations ("right brain"). With just such a subtle shift in the Springboard, note the difference in Hannah's entries below:

> My mother is driving me crazy. She called again tonight, drunk. I told her to call me tomorrow when she can talk intelligently. She cried, I cried. I ended up screaming at her to get control of herself. Then she hung up on me. I have a huge headache. . . .

> Why is my mother driving me crazy? I feel so helpless. I feel like I'm abandoning her when she needs me most. What if she had abandoned me when I needed her for survival? Don't I owe this to her? Here comes the guilt. I'm a lousy daughter!

When you look closely at Springboards, you'll see that they are essentially generic sentences or questions which have a "fill-in-the-blank" aspect. Hannah could have just as easily written, "My boyfriend is driving me crazy" or "My boss is driving me crazy." Or she could have jumped off with "My mother is driving me to Pheonix."

SPRINGBOARDS

Allow Springboards to help you manage your journal time. Do you remember the old television game show "Beat the Clock"? The contestants won prizes if they could complete seemingly impossible stunts in an allocated amount of time. What I didn't realize when I was a kid watching the show is that life is very often a game of "Beat the Clock"—so many tasks, so little time!

I had one of those days recently. Deadline projects were due in three parts of the city; I'd overslept; I had a week's worth of work marked "MUST DO TODAY." In desperation, I grabbed my notebook and wrote a Springboard: "What's the most important thing to do?"

Much to my surprise and annoyance, the answer that immediately appeared was "Write in this journal!" Although at that particular moment it seemed to be the most blatant of time-wasters, I gave myself 15 minutes. The resultant entry was a beautiful prioritizing of my day and included a map of the most efficient automobile route. That Springboard led me into the most productive quarter hour of the day.

QUOTATIONS AS SPRINGBOARDS

Quotations make marvelous Springboards. If you like blank bound books, check at your stationer or bookseller for the softbound blank books that carry a theme throughout their pages. Titles I have seen include *An Artist's Notebook, A Writer's Notebook,* and *A Woman's Notebook.* Each page is illustrated with line drawings and a quotation related to the theme of the book. Dr. Andrea Van Steenhouse, a Denver psychologist and radio talk-show hostess, has published a blank book called *Life Lines* which features drawings of quilt patterns and quotations about psychology and personal growth.

By using the quotation as a Springboard, you'll have a rich, enjoyable opportunity to reflect and philosophize on a variety of topics. You can use song lyrics in the same way—particularly when a snatch of a song is dancing through your mind and won't leave you alone!

K.I.S.S.: KEEP IT SHORT AND SIMPLE

Keep your Springboards short and simple. Compare these two Springboards and decide which would more readily get you in the flow of journal writing:

> I'm concerned that the recent capital investment in machinery will adversely affect profitability in the coming fiscal year, particularly with regard to short-term positioning.
>
> vs
>
> I'm scared I'm going broke!

There's nothing *wrong* with the first one. It just may not be as conducive to "telling the complete truth faster." Simply getting to the point is generally more productive.

Ted, 48, is well-known in his social and professional circles as a silver-tongued orator, never at a loss for words. His fondness for eloquent speeches, however, did not find expression in his journaling. Ted found himself frustrated: in the journal he found himself able to address only day-to-day aspects of his life, and he seemed unable to write deeply about himself and his concerns. One day he tried a sentence-completion Springboard around his feelings. Ted wrote, "I feel left out." That simple opener was the invitation he needed to begin purging a deep and poignant grief.

SPRINGBOARDS
AS JOURNAL ENTRY

In the following example, Rachel used a collection of Springboards to capture the essence of her self-examination in a tongue-in-cheek way. Any one of the questions she asked herself, however, would make an excellent Springboard for further reflection:

Questions

If I give up my doubts and negativity who will I be? If I give up my ACA identity who will be there in its stead? If I embrace my muck will the dirt wash off my arms? If I turn the pinprick of light into a beam of joy will I be blinded by its radiance? If I see God in everything will he look back? If I fall off the path will I get back on? If I start honoring myself with love and respect will my head swell with greatness? If I live in my body will my skin hurt? If I trust without question will I make mistakes? If I show my ignorance will I lose face? If I lose my face will I still exist? If I expose my fears will I die? If I say goodbye will I have to admit my responsibility in the loss? If I admit my strength will it be taken away? If I acknowledge the joy will it turn into foolishness? If I give up my judgments will I float away? If I open my heart will bugs fly in?

TO HELP YOU START

Keep a list of Springboards on one page of your journal. Then, if you ever find yourself with a blank journal page and an equally blank mind, you'll have help at your fingertips.

Here are some Springboards to get you started:

- Today I feel ——— years old. [6? 16? 60?]
- I am excited about . . .
- Three things I want to accomplish [today, this week, this year, in my lifetime] are . . .
- Where am I in the movement of my [life, business, relationship, career, etc.]?
- What's the most important thing to do right now?
- My ideal work environment would include . . .
- How am I feeling right now?
- The most important skill I need for [a task] is . . .
- What resources are available to me?
- How can I best use my resources?
- What I value most in my relationship with ——— is . . .
- How do I feel about [upcoming event]?
- I'm happiest when . . .
- What turns me on?
- What turns me off?
- I'm proud of myself for . . .
- How am I using my power?
- I'm alone, and it's . . .
- Today was a [great, lousy, hectic, etc.] day.
- Why am I feeling so [angry, sad, paranoid, etc.]?
- What do I really want?
- How am I experiencing [joy, indecision, rage, etc.]?
- My biggest [secret, fear, wish, etc.] is . . .

8

CHARACTER SKETCH

**O wad some Pow'r the giftie gie us
To see ourselv's as ithers see us!**

—Robert Burns
"To a Louse"

A Character Sketch is a written description of another person, or even of yourself. It's a very handy technique to use when you're having a conflict with someone, when you want to see how you might be coming across to someone else, or when you want to get to know the different parts of yourself in a more direct and intimate way.

PROJECTION

The people that we draw into our lives are our mirrors. Everyone with whom we have relationships is our teacher; when we love or hate some quality of another person, it is likely that we are loving or hating that same quality in ourselves, even though we may be denying its very existence in our own personality!

This "mirroring" is called *projection*. In the diagram below, something that is really a part of A's personality is denied or not recognized. This is represented by the small, empty box inside the circle. The contents of this box, whatever they may be, are *projected* onto B, and B is seen as having so much of whatever is in the box that it's difficult for A to see anything else.

Projection functions like the "cut and paste" operation in many word processing programs: scissor it from one document, drop it into another document. But the information physically removed from the first document is still lurking in the buffer, even though you can't see it!

A journal Character Sketch of someone who is "pushing your buttons" is an opportunity to look in the mirror. Ask yourself: What about this person so repels or angers me that I am avoiding seeing it in myself?

In Nathaniel Hawthorne's *The Scarlet Letter,* Puritan towns-people, outraged that Hester Prynne has had a love affair with one of their own, brand her an adulteress. The sentence for her

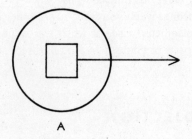 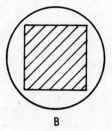

"crime"? She must wear a red "A" on her bosom as a constant reminder that she has sinned.

This is what happens with projection. The townspeople couldn't accept their own sexuality, so they "projected" it onto poor Hester. Her scarlet letter was an external representation of that which her accusers denied internally.

You can also ask yourself: How does this person echo a part of myself that I have *formerly* repressed or denied?

Connie's Character Sketch of Brenda offered an insightful opportunity to bring an old learning to her awareness once again:

Why am I "friends" with Brenda? I just don't like her. She's a self-centered, greedy, needy bitch who expects others to stand at attention to meet her needs, even though she doesn't know what those are half the time. She's deceitful, mean, dishonest and shallow. She's cold and calculating. I can't trust her at all. Why do I stay?

I recognize in Brenda a part of myself from many years ago. I was probably 12 or 13, and I was really mean to people. I was cold and calculating. It lasted for about six months, and then one night my sister and her friend asked me to sleep over with them. I was thrilled and honored. It was the most traumatic night of my life. . . . They spent the entire night until the sun came up telling me what a horrible person I had become. How I was two-faced and phony and mean. I cried all night and all morning and all the next day. And then I hibernated for six months.

I am forever thankful to my sister for what she did for me. She must have been scared to death once she saw the effect it had on me, but it was the right thing to do. Maybe Brenda needs the same kind of help, in a more adult way, of course. . . .

Projection doesn't necessarily imply negativity. It is just as common to deny our positive traits and to "paste" them onto others. Again, a Character Sketch of an idol, hero or heroine, or teacher can help unveil your own potential:

Character Sketch of Mariko

Just being in the same room with her grounds me. I watch her effortless grace and her Oriental smoothness, and I feel refreshed. Invigorated, but in a quiet way. Serenity. She is a goddess surrounded by a bubble of serenity. Nothing can invade it, not war nor poverty nor insult nor air pollution nor the craziness of Western man.

I feel so unfinished when I am with her. Jagged, rough around the edges. I feel young and inept. I feel like a block of stone. Rough. Unfinished. Hard.

And yet in Mariko I see my own possibilities. Or at least I want to think so. Somewhere inside of me there is a goddess, waiting to be born. A sculpture, awaiting the artist's chisel. She is both the artist and the art. I am neither, and yet I wonder . . . could I be? Someday?

SEEING YOURSELF AS OTHERS SEE YOU

Character Sketches are a marvelous way, as the poet Burns says, "to see ourselv's as ithers see us." Try writing a Character Sketch about yourself from the point of view of someone else—perhaps someone with whom you are having difficulty. How does this person perceive you? How do you come across? This can be astonishingly revealing—and perhaps a bit disconcerting, as well!

In Barbara Sher's *Wishcraft: How to Get What You Really Want*, she suggests "investigating" your home as if you were a private detective trying to figure out what sort of person lives in your house:

> Look in the clothes closets, the kitchen cabinets, the book and record shelves. Look at the furniture, the rugs, the curtains, the pictures on the walls, the food in the refrigerator, the colors, the state of clutter or order, the arrangement of space. . . . Would you say that the person who lives here is organized or scatterbrained? Sociable or solitary? Sensual or intellectual?

When you have finished your "investigation," write a Character Sketch of the person who lives in your home (which is, after all, an external metaphor of your personality), as Lily did:

> The exterior of the house is middle-class, proper, taken care of. The front door is a surprise. A giant black-eyed Susan is painted on the door. Is this a sign saying, "Be prepared. I am not really what I appear to be"?
>
> Everything is neat and tidy. Beauty is there in paintings, a collection of whimsical unicorns. The kitchen is open, spacious, functional. The kitchen of a gourmet cook. But the den/study—that's a different story. Everything is dumped in here. The door is closed. What secrets are hidden in here? What is not wanting to be seen, viewed, dealt with in here?
>
> I leave the house knowing that the den must be cleared. The hidden "junk," "stuff," must be filed or tossed. The bills must be paid.

"This certainly tells the story of my life," said Lily, a retired schoolteacher. "The mask, the facade, the shell that I have had around me for so very long. Those who chose not to get to know me saw just the exterior and the kitchen—functional, well-groomed, competent. These people would say, 'Lily can handle it. Lily will know what to do. Lily is strong.' How many times

I wanted to scream that I didn't want to handle anything, I didn't know what to do! But I guess I just dumped all that in the den. Now, little by little, I am shedding the masks. I wonder what bills I still have to pay?"

When you are in situations where you would like to be perceived in a certain way—for instance, a job interview or an important sales call—write a Character Sketch of yourself as you *want* to be seen. Here's an example, written from a receptionist's point of view:

> Wow, who is this guy? He must be applying for the job. I hope they hire him! He's really cute—maybe he's single! I bet he'd be fun to work with. But it's more than that. He looks like he could get the job done. I've never even seen him before five minutes ago, but I like him already. I trust him! He looks honest and sincere. He wouldn't bullshit anybody. He's got power. . . .

GET TO KNOW THE PARTS OF YOURSELF

A hundred or so years ago, before telephones and FAX machines, the wealthy and titled rode around in carriages dropping in on one another. When the gentleman or lady being called on wasn't available, the drop-in would leave a "calling card."

Think of Character Sketches as the "calling cards" of your subpersonalities. (Subpersonalities, you'll recall, are the various parts of yourself—Earth Mother, Scatterbrain, Clown, etc.) In this example—written after a series of dialogues with Gorgo, the Green Monster, who personifies her "trickster" side— Ginger gets an "up-close and personal" look at this part of herself:

CHARACTER SKETCH

Gorgo is a crackling, snorting creature. He can hardly wait to pop out from behind a door and see how frightened I'll be. He sticks out his red tongue at me while he is snorting and jumping up and down. Gorgo's attitude about life is to play games, have fun, be the fool, trip people up who get too inflated or become a "smart ass." His gift to me is to laugh and play. I experience Gorgo in my inner life when I get too caught up in my drama or when I need to lighten up, let go, make a silly face, be a clown. In my outer life I experience his energy when I fall on my face because I got too inflated and took myself too seriously. The more I recognize Gorgo as a part of myself, the more I can release my desire for power trips.

ENHANCE RELATIONSHIPS WITH CHARACTER SKETCHES

Character Sketches make great gifts. Write a Character Sketch of your best friend and enclose it with her birthday card. Write a Character Sketch of each of your children on the first day of the new school year; mount them in a scrapbook.

Gloria got a real shock one day when she sat down to write about her husband (whom she was thinking of divorcing) and emerged with a Character Sketch of a noble, creative, sensitive, hard-working man with whom she was very much in love!

AN ENTRANCE MEDITATION

Find a comfortable position, and close your eyes.
Take a slow, deep breath . . .
    hold it . . . and release it.

Do it again . . .

and again.

Now turn your attention to [the subject of your sketch].

And for now, just observe.

Observe the physical side of [subject].

What do you notice?

What does the physical side seem to say?

Stay there as long as you please . . .

noticing the physical dimension.

And now begin to observe how you feel inside.

What emotions are generated by [subject]?

How do you feel about yourself when you are with [subject]?

And now see if you can tune in to [subject's] feelings, too.

What do you notice?

And as you observe, quietly,

allow yourself to notice more and more . . .

on the physical level, and the emotional . . .

and on the more subtle levels, too.

Notice the energy that surrounds [subject].

See if there is a color or a mood.

Allow thoughts and images and words to fill your awareness.

Stay there as long as you please . . .

And when you are ready,

take a deep breath,

open your eyes,

and begin to write a Character Sketch.

9
CLUSTERING

Clustering . . . is the master key to natural writing.
—Gabriele Lusser Rico
Writing the Natural Way

Clustering is a fun, easy, spontaneous journal technique that helps you access lots of information very quickly. Sometimes called Mind Mapping or Webbing, Clustering has enjoyed popularity as a management tool in business and is perhaps best known for its uses in brainstorming and project management.

As a journal tool, though, Clustering does these and more. It also helps integrate the left and right hemispheres of the brain by drawing from characteristics of each. On the "right brain" side, Clustering generates an easy flow of ideas in random sequence. On the "left brain" side, it provides a structure from which information can be easily organized.

To begin, write a key word or phrase in the middle of the page and draw a circle around it. Then begin to free-associate. Spin thoughts off of other thoughts in single words or short phrases. Circle each one and connect it with a line to the one before it. When a new association occurs to you, go back to the central word and begin a new epicenter. Go all over the page. Continue to work the cluster outward until you have exhausted your immediate possibilities, or until you feel an internal shift from the randomness of association to a sense of clarity or direction.

When you feel such a shift occur, begin to write about the ideas generated by the cluster. You're likely to be surprised by the clarity, quickness, and grace with which your thoughts come together after a Clustering exercise. For example, Ginger's cluster on "power" gave her important insights into the correlation between her personal power and her personal freedom:

> Today I am introduced to my power, not a power over someone but my personal power—who I really am, not what I acquired as a role or picked up along the way as an affectation. Hooray for coming into my own, finding myself. That's power, freedom. This clearly shows a pattern. Half of the clusters end up with the word freedom! Is it possible that by owning my power I gain freedom?

WHEN TO USE CLUSTERING

Clustering is a very time-efficient journal technique. Because the creation of the cluster itself is best done spontaneously,

CLUSTERING

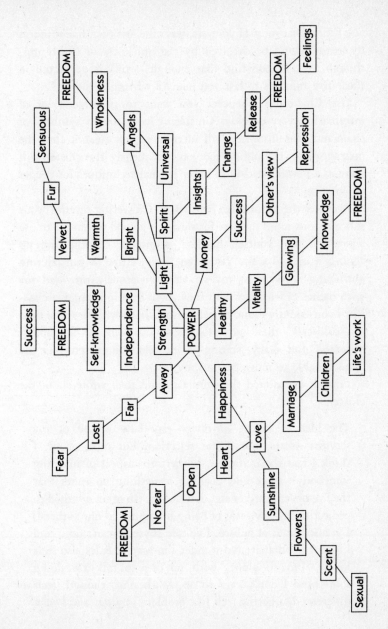

you'll find that most of your clusters take less than five minutes to create. Don't be deceived by the quickness of Clustering, though. You'll soon find that enough "stuff" is generated in those five minutes to last you many a writing session!

Use Clustering whenever you want to generate a lot of information very quickly. Clustering your dream symbols or characters, for instance, will often give you insight into the messages they're holding for you. Frequently the cluster will serve as a natural lead-in to other journal techniques for deeper exploration.

Because the associative nature of Clustering invites your subconscious mind to come forward, it's a good technique to use when you find yourself blocked, stumped, or otherwise up against a mental wall. Years ago, when I first began offering journaling workshops, my students generously provided me with names of friends whom they thought might enjoy a class. But I consistently found myself immobilized when it came time to "cold-call" these prospect lists. I would sit for hours, miserable and shaky, staring at the telephone receiver in my hand, unable to move beyond my fear.

Finally, I clustered the word *sales* and then wrote about the cluster:

> The idea of selling *anything*—especially myself or my services—scares me. I fear rejection, but most of all, I think I fear the irritating, bothersome aspect of invading somebody's space and pushing something on them that they've never heard of and don't want. (In other words, I'm projecting my own fear of being manipulated onto others!) I'm also afraid of failure. I've told myself I can't do it and I'm not good at it. No wonder I'm scared! Sales also feels lonely. I'm all alone, with no one to talk to, doing something I don't want to do. Marketing, though, feels different. Marketing feels like problem solving, and I *know*

I'm good at that. So all I need to do is switch my headset from sales to marketing! (P.S. Three days later: it worked!)

Clustering is an excellent technique for work projects or school papers. The fluid format allows you to make a nonlinear outline from which you can organize a more formal outline or proposal. You'll find that a paper or report virtually writes itself from the information in the cluster. (See figure 3 for the Cluster from which this paragraph and the next were written!)

When you are working on a large project, try putting butcher or mural paper on your office wall. Cluster each section of the project. From this picture you can create time lines, delegate tasks, and monitor deadlines. You can color-code your wall cluster with highlighter pens and stick notes on individual circles to help you stay on top of all of your project's details.

WRITING THE NATURAL WAY

An excellent resource for detailed information on the process and applications of Clustering is Dr. Gabriele Lusser Rico's *Writing the Natural Way.* The author has done extensive research

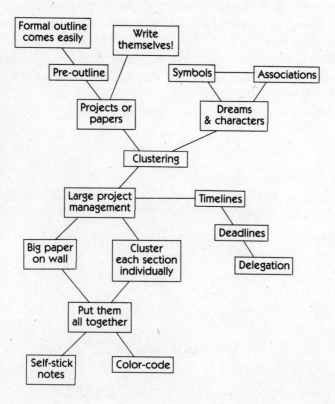

on brain hemispheres and creativity. Her book is a gold mine of exercises, techniques, and tips to unleash creative expression and "natural writing" through Clustering.

10

CAPTURED

MOMENTS

A Captured Moment allows the truth to emerge in a magical way.

**—student of Journaling As a
Therapeutic Tool**

A bedtime story on Grandma's lap . . . the birth of a child . . . an exquisite autumn leaf . . . a surprise visit by your dearest friend . . . a parent's funeral . . . catching crawdads in the creek . . . a breathtaking sunset . . . the heart-wrench of a broken love affair . . . your first pony ride . . .

These tiny moments of intimacy, yearning, beauty, despair, exhilaration—these are the moments to capture and hold forever in your heart.

The Captured Moments journal technique allows you to

celebrate and savor, preserving in prose the glory and anguish, the serenity and sorrow, the pleasure and pain of your life.

A Captured Moment is a frozen morsel of time. Exactly as a camera shutter captures a split second of infinity on film, so does a Captured Moment preserve an instant of feeling and sensation.

Captured Moments are best written from the senses. This technique allows you to pull out all the stops with your creativity, describing in detail the sounds, sights, smells, and feelings of a moment in time and space:

The cab plods its way through Manhattan's sweaty streets. The air inside is foul with cigarette smoke; the air outside is worse. My mood is as dingy as the grime-caked taxi window. I am hot. I am depressed. I am alone. I feel as dead as the stagnant air. Outside of this taxi, there is life. There is a sidewalk where winos puke, hookers strut, druggers score. It is a sidewalk of despair, a taxi of despair, a city of despair. Perhaps it is a world and a galaxy and a universe of despair.

And then I see her. She is maybe eight years old. Her skin is glossy black, her hair in a hundred tiny braids sticking like antenna from her head. She wears a screaming yellow sunsuit. And she is flying. She has found the only patch of sunlight in the borough, a determined beam that peeks down the shaft between two tenements. Face turned upward to greet the welcome sun, eyes squinched shut, rapturous gap-toothed grin, she is soaring off the sidewalk, legs kicked up behind her. She is eight years old, and she has a bright yellow sunsuit, and there is sunshine on her face, and she leaps for joy because for this tiny moment, all is right with her world.

And suddenly, all is right with mine, as well.

"I wrote this Captured Moment in the taxicab," reports Allyson, a magazine writer. "I dug through my purse, frantically searching for a scrap of paper, then pounded on the plexiglass panel that separated me from the driver. He was Lebanese, I think—I had a hard time making him understand what I needed. Finally he handed back his clipboard and a receipt pad, and I scribbled it as fast as I could. To this day, when I am feeling the angst of despair, I close my eyes and remember that beautiful child, and I know that somewhere in this situation there is joy."

And so one of the beauties of a Captured Moment is its ability to bring you *back* to a place of awareness. Similarly, another beauty is the ability to help *create* a place of awareness, as this Captured Moment did for Laura, who went into a program for alcohol recovery shortly after writing it:

> I poured a tumbler of Dubonnet wine, sweet, thick, rich red, clinging to the side of the glass the way aperitifs do, and I added a wedge of lemon to cut the sweetness, and I drank it fast—relaxing—relishing the release in my tense body—gratefully. Still wearing my coat, purse over my shoulder, one shoe kicked off, grocery bag on the floor where I dropped it, I'm pouring another glass of this beautiful red liquid, squeezing another wedge of lemon— licking my fingers so the tartness bursts in my head—and winding down. The pain in my right side easing—and words fill my mind and arm and spill onto the paper as I drink deeply, deeply drink.

"I was both horrified and aroused at the sensuousness of my drinking patterns," Laura confessed. "When it was there in black and white, I realized I was having a love affair with my wine. That scared me. I quit drinking almost immediately. Recovery has been slow, and I can't say I've been one hundred percent in my recovery process. But I'm on the right track. And I'm finding other, healthier outlets for my sensuality."

CAPTURED MOMENTS

Much like snapshots in a photo album, Captured Moments can be used to preserve a precious memory for the future:

I saw you for the first time today, my little one. The doctor hooked me up to an elaborate claptrap of technology—I giggled, thinking how decidedly unromantic it felt to be sprawled on an examining table contemplating the miracle of birth with wires running every which way. But then, suddenly, there you were, on a television screen, a fragile butterfly floating gracefully on a cloud of gray, and my heart stopped for just an instant and then filled to overflowing with the purest love, the holiest dedication. . . . I saw you for the first time today, my first-born child, and I knew at that moment that I shall love you for eternity.

"The experience of that sonogram will live forever in my heart," Julie reminisced. "My baby was born beautiful and healthy four months later. She is the joy of my life. I've started a 'baby book' of Captured Moments, and this is the first entry."

CAPTURED CREATIVITY

The creativity inherent in a Captured Moment can unlock the subtle nuances of the experience which may otherwise go unnoticed. During one extravagantly glorious Colorado October, fully half of my students turned in autumn leaves labeled Captured Moments! Many elaborated in prose, as Sally did:

The poplar trees show autumn on the edges, fringes of yellow reminding me of other autumns, other places, other colors, varying onsets and feelings. Trees I recall. Fragrances of other times, other lives. Golden to red to burgundy, exotic orange to salmon against lavender or tangerine skies. Autumn, the time of new beginnings, is my favorite season. I welcome you into my world one more year.

Poetry is often a worthy and wonderful vehicle for your Captured Moments. If you haven't written poetry since high school and don't know the first thing about it, try it anyway. Your journal is a forgiving, nonjudgmental place to flex your creative muscles, and the results can be quite rewarding. The following Captured Moment could have just as easily been written in prose, but the haunting, raw beauty of the outer world contrasted with the warm, cozy intimacy of the inner world is captured eloquently in poetic form:

Windbreak

The night of the snowstorm
The stars disappeared.
We heard wind rattle windows
And moan down the chimney.
Ice-heavy snow lashed the house.
The dogs whined to come inside,
But the cats were gone
To warmer regions they alone can find.
I imagined calves
Climbing snow-drifted fences
To find the snow that might be whiter,
While horses in the barn leaned together,
Content with only one warm side.

And we
Found old lanterns and candles,
Lit the fireplace, stoked the wood stove,
And sat and listened to snow-muffled wind
Encircle us with crystals.

I watched you listen.
In the golden glow of lamplight
I saw in your face new repose,
In your eyes satisfaction.
Tomorrow we'll shovel out.
The drifts will shine—dunes of pearl.
You held my hand,
We murmured warm reflections
And waited out the storm.

"There was something so poignant, so intimate about that night," Lois remembered. "It was one of the few times in the latter years of my marriage when my husband and I were truly unified. It was a moment worth capturing."

The late Anaïs Nin is a master of Captured Moments. The seven volumes of her published adult diaries are illuminated with beautiful descriptions, many of which are vignettes that offer insight and clarification into painful or problematic situations. The little, innocuous events of her days turned into opportunities to make statements about the world around her, her personal philosophy, and her triumphs and tragedies. Ms. Nin holds a well-deserved place in history and literature as one of the premier diarists of this or any other time, and her works cannot be recommended highly enough to any journal writer. Savor the power and simplicity of an entry dated July 1935:

Reality. When you are in the heart of a summer day as inside a fruit, looking down at your lacquered toenails, at the white dust on your sandals gathered from quiet somnolescent streets. Looking at the sun expanding under your dress and between your legs, looking at the light polishing the silver bracelets, smelling the bakery odors . . . watching the cars rolling by, filling with blonde women taken from pictures in *Vogue*, then you see suddenly the old cleaning woman with her burnt, scarred, iron-colored face, and you read about the man who was cut into pieces, and in front of you now stops the half-body of a man resting on a flat cart with small wheels.

ENTRANCE MEDITATION

Ready to write a Captured Moment? Remember to focus on the *sensory details* of the event. This is a place to write with flourish. Sprinkle your Captured Moments lavishly with descriptive words. Let them flow out of your pen. And enjoy yourself!

Find a comfortable position, and close your eyes.
Take a slow, deep breath . . .
    hold it . . . and release it.
    Do it again . . . and again.
Now imagine your mind as a movie screen.
And on this screen,
    allow memories to float freely . . .
    one at a time . . .
    memories of moments you wish to capture.
Watch the memories float across
    the movie screen of your mind . . .
    one at a time . . .
    noticing each one in turn.
Now choose one memory to write about. . . .
    Allow one memory to return to the screen
    and stay there.
And now, step into the movie screen.
Look down and see yourself in this memory. . . .
    Notice what you are wearing . . .
    how it feels to be in your body. . . .
    Recreate the feeling of being in this memory.
And now add in the details of the scene.

CAPTURED MOMENTS

Take your paintbrush and add in the colors.
Listen for the sounds around you. . . .
   Notice if there is anyone else in the scene. . . .
   Recreate every detail of the scene . . .
   the smells . . .
   the tastes . . .
   the textures. . . .
Return again to the feelings inside.
Allow yourself to fully experience . . .
   all of the sensations . . .
   both outer and inner . . .
   that you associate with this memory.
Stay there as long as you like . . .
   fully participating
   in the re-creation of this memory . . .
   reliving every nuance,
   every detail,
   of this time. . . .
And when you are ready,
   open your eyes,
   take a deep breath,
   and begin to write a Captured Moment.

11

DIALOGUE

In the diary I can keep track of the two faces of reality.

—Anaïs Nin

The Dialogue technique is the Swiss army knife of the journal toolbox. A marvel of flexibility, Dialogue can take you into or through nearly any journal situation you can imagine. It is the technique of choice of many experienced journalers and is a key component of Dr. Progoff's Intensive Journal™ workshop.

Although Dr. Progoff is generally credited with developing journal Dialogues (*At a Journal Workshop* devotes six chapters to the subject), the dialogue format is a popular technique in many modern psychotherapeutic genres, including Gestalt "empty chair" work, Jungian active imagination, and the subpersonality work of psychosynthesis.

Whether used in the journal or in a therapy session with a trained guide, a Dialogue follows basically the same form: it is an exchange between you and someone or something else, where you play both parts. In the journal, a Dialogue is a written conversation. On the page, it looks like a movie or theater script:

ME: You're all very small.
FEARS: Fears don't grow, they multiply.

Understandably, this format feels unnatural at first, and it may take a little practice to get into the rhythm of speaking for both you and your Dialogue partner in turn. If your first few Dialogues don't produce the results that you're after, stay with it. You weren't able to tie your shoes perfectly the first few times you tried, either.

Progoff's Intensive Journal™ method teaches five types of Dialogue in the Dialogue Dimension section:

- Dialogue with Persons
- Dialogue with Events and Circumstances
- Dialogue with Works
- Dialogue with the Body
- Dialogue with Societies

To this list I would add four more:

- Dialogue with Emotions/Feelings
- Dialogue with Material Objects/Possessions
- Dialogue with Subpersonalities/Symbols
- Dialogue with Resistance/Block

And developed by Dr. Progoff, in a class by itself, is

- Dialogue with Inner Wisdom

ENTERING THE DIALOGUE

No matter what or whom you choose as your Dialogue partner, you're likely to have better results with a little advance preparation:

• **Create a pleasant environment.** Make sure that you have the privacy and space that you need. Try out your pen to make sure that it feels comfortable; have a spare handy. Check your notebook to make sure you won't run out of pages. Pour yourself a glass of water or a cup of tea. Light a candle; burn some incense. Do whatever you need to ensure your optimum comfort.

• **Give yourself plenty of time.** The most effective Dialogues tend to unfold in cycles or waves of writing and reflection. Schedule an hour for your first few Dialogues. This may be too much time or not enough, but at least you'll have a barometer for the future.

• **Start with an entrance meditation.** Reflect on the relationship you currently have with your Dialogue partner, how the relationship feels to you, any questions you would like to ask, the statements you would like to make. (A generic entrance meditation, which can be adapted for your individual purposes, is included at the end of this chapter.)

• **Warm up with other techniques.** After the meditation, you may want to write a Character Sketch of your Dialogue partner, or a list of questions you'd like to ask. Progoff's Dialogue method includes writing a focusing statement about your current position within the relationship and a list of

Steppingstones for the Dialogue partner. Any of these techniques, or others, can help you focus more clearly on the energy surrounding the situation or Dialogue partner.

If you are dialoguing with something that isn't an object or another human being, personify your Dialogue partner in some way. Not only is it difficult to have a conversation with an abstraction, but Progoff points out that "when we perceive the [Dialogue partner] as a person, there can be a relationship of equals between us."

• Allow yourself to feel temporarily uncomfortable. It is perfectly natural to feel as if you are "making it up." You *are* making it up! But out of everything you *could* be writing, this is what you *are* writing. Let it be okay that you might be making it up. It is also perfectly natural to feel silly the first few times you have a conversation with your big toe. Let this be okay as well. The discomfort only lasts a little while, and most journalers come to have a great respect and affection for Dialogues.

• Respect the silence. Sometimes your questions or responses will formulate as words in your mind; sometimes they will flow out of your pen seemingly without volition. Write them, either way. When you come to a natural pause in the Dialogue, close your eyes and wait in silence for the next question or answer. It is often helpful to quietly ask yourself, "What does my heart say?"

• Exit gracefully. The fact that you have come to a natural pause does not necessarily mean the Dialogue is completed. If the Dialogue does not resume after sitting in silence, reread what you have written; often you will spontaneously begin again when you come to the end. Any time you feel you are approaching completion with a Dialogue, you can ask, "Is there anything more?" And it's a nice touch to thank your Dialogue partner and ask permission to contact him/her/it again for another conversation:

Dialogue with Bald Man (Dream Character)

ME: Is there anything else?

HIM: Not right now. I think you've got plenty to work with.

ME: Thanks for the insight. Can we talk again?

HIM: Sure. Do you want it here, or in a dream?

ME: I'd like to know I can access you consciously, through my journal.

HIM: You got it!

• **Have fun.** Some of your Dialogue partners will take on quirky personalities that can range from annoying to amusing. This will unfold as the process unfolds. Katherine dialogued with her chronically tight jaw and found that it took on the personality of a large black woman who exuded earthiness and competence. "You gotta get out there, girl, and *say what's on your mind!*" her "jaw" told her. "Quit bitin' back those words!" Expecting the unexpected is a delightful part of the Dialogue process.

• **Trust the process.** You may get answers and insights that seem to come from nowhere. The place they are coming from is most likely your subconscious, unconscious, or superconscious mind. The Dialogue technique is a way to bring this information to consciousness, where it may feel unfamiliar, strange, or unsettling. Trust the process. Trust the process. Trust. Trust. Trust.

PERSONS

This Dialogue can be with anyone in your life—past, present, or future; living or dead or not yet born. It is *not* necessary that the person you choose to dialogue with be actively in your life. Journal Dialogues with a deceased parent or the lover who walked out on you can be a key factor in completing unfinished business.

The Dialogue with Persons provides insight into your own behavior and can help to clarify a clouded position. Barbara's Dialogue with her estranged husband, who had filed for divorce with no explanation, helped her not only to ventilate her anger but also find direction for the future:

ME: It's just like every other situation in our marriage. You always get your way! You always get to call the shots! Well, what about ME? What about MY needs?

HIM: You never let me know you had any needs! How can you fault me? You acted like your whole life revolved around taking care of me. You sacrificed too much of yourself for me.

ME: I won't make that mistake again! I'm going to take care of myself, by God, and pity the man who tries to come between me and myself!

HIM: Good for you. It's time you realized that you're worth more than I was able to give you.

Similarly, this technique is extremely useful in helping you see another's point of view. Annette wrote an imaginary conversation with her friend George, who had sought her counsel on his pending marriage. An only child, George had lost his father to a sudden death a few years before; his mother had just recovered from a near-fatal illness. In the Dialogue, Annette expressed her concern that George did not seem happy with his choice of partner:

ME: Sometimes you act like you don't even like Sandra, much less love her. I can't figure out why you want to commit yourself to a loveless marriage. Does this have anything to do with your mother? And your father's death?

G: My mother's illness really shook me up. You don't know what it feels like to know that someday, maybe soon, you won't have any family in the world—that you won't belong.

ME: So you're willing to get married to have that security, even if it's a struggle sometimes?

G. Yes. Sandra is a good woman. We'll have our problems, but we'll make it work.

ME: You'll have my full support.

EVENTS/CIRCUMSTANCES

A popular notion today is that we create our own reality; everything that happens to us manifests out of our conscious thought. It might be more helpful to say that everything we manifest comes out of our *unconscious* thought, because it is only when our will is aligned with our deepest desire that the desire comes forth in form.

It is also arguably true that we draw into our lives the players who will help us act out whatever life script we're starring in this season. (They, of course, drew us into theirs for the same reason, so we're supporting actors in their life scripts, too.) Think about this for a while, and you'll get a sense of the sheer numbers of geometrically perfect Busby Berkeley dances going on simultaneously.

DIALOGUE

Some of the events and circumstances in your life have appeared because your will was aligned with your unconscious desire. Weddings and pregnancies, for example, might fall into this category. Some events and circumstances (maybe death, divorce, or abortion) are drawn in because you're a supporting player in someone else's show. Some of your events and circumstances show up because your unconscious desire and your conscious desire don't match. High drama (getting fired, going bankrupt, having your heart broken) is often the result. And then there are the biggies—the earthquake in South America, war in the Middle East—where we are all just extras, like the battlefield scene in *Gone with the Wind*.

Dialogue with the various events and circumstances in your life. Ask what the lesson is and how you can learn it gracefully. Find out where your cue cards are. If an event (such as getting passed over for a raise) is a result of holding an outdated belief system (such as, "I'm not worth that much money"), try using the Dialogue with Events to clarify your unconscious desire.

WORKS

"Artists get unstuck by getting in touch with the source of their inspiration," writes Progoff, and the Dialogue with Works allows you to develop a friendship with the Muse.

Dialogue with Works partners can include:

- *Your current income-producing job,* especially when you are feeling frustrated, blocked, uncertain, or ready for a change
- *Your future income-producing job,* especially when you are comtemplating a career change
- *Your career to date.* What sort of a "personality" does your career have? Where does it see itself in its life cycle? How does it feel about itself? What does it want from you?

- *Your hobbies or leisure-time activities.* Are they feeling neglected? What would they like to be doing with you?
- *Your creative works.* Dialogue with those works into which you pour energy with an emotional commitment (these may include your garden, collection of miniatures, sewing machine, oil painting, book of poetry, woodwork, piano—the list goes on and on):

ME: We're on the home stretch. . . .

BOOK: You're doing a lovely job. You can be very proud of yourself.

ME: Will I get you finished by Monday?

BOOK: Yes, I believe so. I think you'll push straight through. Next week, though, I want you to begin eating better and getting more exercise. You've been neglecting yourself.

ME: I love you very much. Talk to you later.

- *The Muse.* Dialogue with the source of your creative energy and inspiration. Ask the Muse how you can access her. Let her help you design creative rituals for your work.
- *Your work.* Your life's work. Your heart's deepest desire. The reason you were put on the planet. The way you will leave your thumbprint on the world. The work you can do with complete joy and alignment. Ask how you can get started. Invite your life's work to make itself known to you.

THE BODY

Our bodies are the vehicles through which we experience life. Christ taught that the body was the temple of God. A healthy body that functions efficiently is a valuable resource for you; it allows you to do what you want to do.

DIALOGUE

Since they come only one per customer, it's important to know how to communicate with it! The innate wisdom of the body speaks in often direct metaphor, and a written Dialogue enables you to find out what your body is trying to teach you.

A few winters ago, I slipped on a patch of ice and landed on a sharp rock, smack on my tailbone. Ouch! Because it was so painful, I had an excuse to procrastinate on a project that I didn't think I was experienced or "good" enough to do in the first place. The longer I procrastinated, the crazier I got, and my tailbone just wouldn't stop hurting:

ME: Hey, tailbone, what's going on?
TB: Get off your butt.
ME: Huh??
TB: You're not going to get anything done as long as you sit around waiting for somebody to rescue you. . . .

After an exasperated tirade, my tailbone got in a parting shot:

TB: Your life would quit being such a pain in the ass if you'd just *do* something.

I was so astonished by this Dialogue that I immediately leaped from my chair—and realized that my tailbone only hurt when I was "sitting around"!

Try a Dialogue with:

- a body part or organ
- an illness, injury, or "event" (e.g., surgery)
- an addiction or habit (e.g., alcohol, cigarettes, sugar)
- allergies
- sexuality
- body subpersonalities (Health, Thin Self, Fat Self, the Addict)

- foods and nutrition
- pain (*always* a messenger!)

SOCIETY

Progoff defines *societies* as "those aspects of our experience in which we draw upon our cultural and historical rather than our individual sources for the conduct of our lives." In other words, the Dialogue with Society is a dialogue with "that part of myself that is there before I am." Your race, tribe, religion, ethnic group, clan, political party, socioeconomic class, neighborhood—these are all influencers that are larger than you, and no matter what choices you make in adulthood, you can never alter the societies into which you were born.

Several years ago, a television miniseries based on Alex Haley's *Roots* took the nation by storm. (*Roots* was a genealogical drama that traced Mr. Haley's ancestors back to the village in Africa from which they were first captured into slavery.) For many Americans, it was the first time they had thought about where they might have come from, who their ancestors might have been, what customs and rituals they might be heir to. To dialogue with societies is to glimpse the simultaneous uniqueness and collectiveness of each individual; it provides an opportunity to deepen your awareness of the larger ongoing movement of your life. Who were you before you were you?

In *At a Journal Workshop,* Progoff observes:

> Individuals have chosen to do their dialogues not only with the special social groups from which they are descended and with which they have their immediate affiliation, but with mankind as a whole. They are thus expressing their intimation of the fact that the possibilities of a person's social identifications are not limited to the proximate

groups of birth or environment. They may reach to larger, universal or global units, such as those envisioned by Teilhard de Chardin, Aurobindo, and other philosophers. By the light of such visions, it may be very relevant to establish a dialogue relationship with One World, a transnational government, or a vision of Utopian society in which humanity is united. . . . with the process of evolution by which our species has evolved, or with the seed of humanity that carries the potential of the human species.

When you dialogue with a society, use as your Dialogue partner a person who represents the society for you. As an example, if you are dialoguing with the Catholic Church, you might want to dialogue with your parish priest, the nun who rapped your knuckles in parochial school, or the pope.

EMOTIONS/FEELINGS

Energy isn't "bad" or "good," it's just energy. Sometimes it's the *intensity* of the energy that makes us want to place a value judgment on it; a soaking rainstorm in the drought-stricken Midwest is cause for prayers of thanksgiving, while a hurricane off the Gulf Coast is cause for prayers of mercy. But each is made up of the same meteorological energy.

When you think of emotions as "energy in motion" (E-motion), you can begin to sense that feelings might not be "good" or "bad," either. But we place labels on our feelings: happiness is good; anger is bad; guilt is normal; love is the ultimate; hate is unmentionable. No wonder there is so much about our own feelings that we don't know!

Think about the family you grew up in. Which emotions were you expected to feel? Which were encouraged? Which were frowned upon? Which were grounds for excommunication?

The feelings that you have rarely or never allowed yourself to experience can be mystifying; sometimes it's hard to even put a name on them. Let the Dialogue serve as a "reality check":

ME: I'm not even sure I'd know you if I felt you.

LOVE: Describe how you felt last Saturday in the mountains.

ME: Good. I felt peaceful, warm, connected with nature. It was a good feeling.

LOVE: How did you feel about Debbie?

ME: Warm. Close. Happy to be sharing the day with her. Glad we're back together.

LOVE: That was me.

Remember to personify the partner in an entrance meditation, or try drawing the emotion before you begin the Dialogue. Blythe drew a picture of a wild animal with its foot caught in a trap to represent her grief. At the end of the Dialogue, her grief told her:

GRIEF: You must trust that I don't want to kill you. But the more I pile up inside you, the less room there is for anything else. Release me! Let me go!

Try Dialogues with:

- Anger, hate, or rage
- Love
- Joy, ecstasy, or bliss
- Grief, sadness, or pain
- Guilt or shame
- Fear, terror, or horror

- Insecurity or uncertainty
- Passion

MATERIAL OBJECTS/POSSESSIONS

Progoff stresses that a Dialogue must be considered "meaningful as experienced from an interior point of view," and thus it is quite likely that if you dialogue with a random object or possession, you won't get remarkable results. (On the other hand, as an experiment, I once had a class dialogue with the chairs they were sitting on, and just about everyone felt he or she attained insight. This lends credibility to the idea that there is meaning where you seek it.)

The Dialogue with Possessions can be useful in helping you uncover the symbology or underlying belief system you associate with your material goods. Money Dialogues can be particularly revealing; Mickey attributes her Dialogue with "turning my relationship with money around 180 degrees":

MICKEY: Hello! You're Money, aren't you?

MONEY: Yes. Do I look like what you expected?

MICKEY: No, I didn't realize you had so many aspects to you. I guess I always saw you as something to pay bills with and do what was absolutely necessary, but not as a wonderful, fun person.

MONEY: You can see why I didn't particularly want to hang out with you! You made me feel like such a drudge.

MICKEY: I am sorry!

MONEY: Do you think we could spend more time together? And have fun together?

MICKEY: Yes, I think that you are very attractive.

"This Dialogue showed me more about my state of mind toward money than any conversation or thinking process ever had," Mickey told me, with a laugh. "Now, every time I spend money in an 'oh, so responsible' mind-set, I can see this little green man at my elbow feeling unappreciated. I still spend the money in the same way, but I do it with a light, loving, generous attitude. It makes all the difference!"

SUBPERSONALITIES AND SYMBOLS

Sometimes the best Dialogues are with parts of yourself that are clamoring for attention.

Sally was awakened in the middle of the night by a dream of an "alter ego," Bolivar Sockwads. She described him in her journal as "a blustering bumbler with a handlebar moustache. He has been bumbling through my life lately, causing me to trip on level surfaces, overshoot chair seats, and spill cups of coffee. I think Sockwads appears in my life when too many have-to's get in the way of my want-to's."

ME: You woke me up, Socks. Why did I wake up thinking of you?

SOCKS: Because I don't like this bedtime ritual. Dennis says (grumpy voice), "Are you going to bed soon?" and you say (squeaky voice), "Pretty soon." What you really want to say is, "I'll go to bed when I damn well please. I want to stay up and do something fun for myself."

ME: I don't want the turmoil that would cause.

SOCKS: We need a vacation away from everyone. Go see Madelyn, sit in her hot tub. Find some fun friends. Do something unprofound for a change. We need some fun and a belly laugh. What ever happened to your idea that humor can cure? Why aren't you having more fun? When was the last time you laughed? *Really* laughed. Do something ridiculous before I die in here!

ME: If I do, will you stop being such a klutz?

SOCKS: Yeah. I just wanted to get your attention.

ME: Okay. We'll do something fun tomorrow. Now can I get some sleep?

SOCKS: Sure. Happy dreams!

Giving voice to this "Bolivar Sockwads" part of herself, the part that wants to be silly and have fun, allowed Sally to put into perspective the importance of relaxation in her life.

Dream characters and symbols can be treated in the same way as subpersonalities, because their function is to help you learn more about the various subpersonalities or dimensions of your life that they represent. Get to know your subpersonalities, dream characters, and symbols by asking questions like these:

- What part of me do you represent?
- How can I recognize you?
- When and how do you want expression?
- What is your healthy purpose in my life?
- How do you act out or misbehave when I don't pay attention to you?
- How can I integrate you into my Self?
- What can I learn from you?
- How can we work together?

RESISTANCE/BLOCK

When you're stuck, acknowledge it and work with it. The way out is in, as Linda found out:

ME: Wall, I'm up against you again. You're a thin aluminum steel wall that is perfectly smooth—no hand or footholds. I can't climb over you, I can't get around you. No windows. How can I get through?

WALL: I don't want you to get through. That's why I'm so tall and wide.

ME: I realize that. But it's time for me to move on. I know that you're protecting me, and I appreciate it. You've been very helpful; you've kept me from getting hurt. But I think I'm strong enough now. Don't you?

WALL: You're much stronger than you were, that's true.

ME: Am I strong enough?

WALL: Maybe for a little bit at a time. Not for all at once. That would be overwhelming.

ME: Surely you have a window somewhere. May I peek through it and get a tiny look at what's on the other side?

WALL: Yes, I guess that would be all right.

INNER WISDOM DIALOGUE

The Inner Wisdom Dialogue is one of the greatest gifts available to the sincere journaler. "Man does indeed know intuitively more than he rationally understands," writes Progoff, and the Inner Wisdom Dialogue is designed specifically to "establish a dialogue relationship with the quality of *knowledge beyond understanding* that becomes present to us at . . . depth." Dialoguing with God, your Higher Power, your spirit guides, or any other expression of your inner wisdom can be a beautiful, spiritual, lyrical experience.

Giving God a voice in your life can lead to reassuring awarenesses and insights, as Michael discovered:

ME: Hi, God, it's me.

GOD: Hey, Michael, haven't heard from you in a while.

ME: Yeah, trying different life-styles and such.

GOD: Know all about it.

ME: I'm at a stage where I need help. I want to break through. I want to know.

GOD: Why do you need to know? Isn't your trust strong enough?

ME: I guess not. I don't trust you, I don't trust me. I know I have all the answers. I just can't get to them right now. I'm in pain. My soul hurts.

GOD: Mike, you're going through a cleansing period. You need to flush out a lot of the old to make room for the new. So go ahead and let go as you need to, and hang on as you need to, too. You can't rush it. I'm with you, and you'll get there in your own good time. Hang in there!

My first encounter with the Inner Wisdom Dialogue came in a Transformational Journal Workshop led by Eiko Michi, a student of and former trainer for Progoff. Ten days earlier, my husband had died. In shock, in pain, and in childlike terror of the unknown that loomed before me, I asked for guidance from my inner wisdom:

ME: My heart is open to your wisdom. Speak to me of what will happen next. What season of my life will unfold?

FW: As the leaves turn and fall, so will your heartache.

ME: And then the winter chill?

IW: The winter chill is outside only. Inside, you will be warm, and safe.

ME: Please talk to me. Please tell me what to do.

IW: Listen to the symphony around you. Talk to the quiet voice inside. Surrounding you are harmony and love; they protect you like a shield. You need not feel guilt or obligation. They are there for you because you have earned them; their price has been high in tears and pain. But as you have done for your brother, let your brother now do for you. Then be very grateful, and fill the well once more.

ME: Is there anything else?

IW: Seek the truth. Seek it actively; do not wait for it to find you. And question not that which you cannot explain. In time, it will unfold.

ENTRANCE MEDITATION

This entrance meditation can serve as an entree into any of the Dialogues discussed in this chapter. If you are dialoguing with something other than a person, remember to create a visual image or representation of your Dialogue partner. Feel free to change the locale to a mountaintop, a meadow, a forest, or any other setting that will enhance your imagery.

Find a comfortable position, and close your eyes.
Take a slow, deep breath . . .

hold it . . . and release it.

Do it again . . .

and again.

Now imagine yourself walking on a beach.

It's a warm day . . . just a hint of a breeze.

The sun feels good against your cheek.

You can hear the gulls.

The waves tickle your bare feet.

You're on your way to a meeting with [Dialogue partner].

Notice how you feel inside as you prepare to meet [partner].

Notice any sensations in your body . . .

and any feelings you may be having, too.

And as you walk down the beach, you can see [partner] in the distance . . . waiting for you.

You can barely make out some physical details.

Like, how big [partner] is.

And whether [partner] is man, or woman, or animal, or other.

Check in with your feelings.

Now you're almost there. [Partner] is waiting for you.

You're close enough now to notice the details of [partner's] appearance.

And you can sense [partner's] mood and attitude.

Notice the expression on [partner's] face . . .

[his/her/its] posture . . . attitude . . . mood.

Notice your own mood and attitude as well.

Take as long as you want to communicate with [partner] nonverbally . . .

and when you are ready, you can say hello.

[Partner] will say hello.

And then you may ask any questions you wish to ask,

knowing you will receive an honest answer . . .

and you may make any statements you wish to make,
knowing you will be heard.
You and [partner] will continue this dialogue . . .
back and forth . . .
asking and responding in turn . . .
until it is complete.
So take as much time as you'd like . . .
and when you are ready . . .
take a deep breath,
open your eyes,
and begin to write your Dialogue.

1 2
LISTS

Tell me to what you pay attention, and I will tell you who you are.

—José Ortega y Gassett

Quick! Write a list of the lists you most frequently write:

1. _____

2. _____

3. _____

4. _____

5. _____

If you're like most people, your "list of lists" reads something like this:

1. Things to do
2. Grocery shopping
3. Christmas cards to send
4. Things you want for your birthday
5. Did you even get a fifth on your "list of lists"? Many people don't!

In our society, we most often use lists as a time-management or memory-jogging tool. There's certainly nothing wrong with this task-oriented approach; lists have done long and faithful service to help keep us organized and on top of the multitude of details inherent in any busy life. But journal lists—ah! That's another species!

JOURNAL LISTS OF 100

Journal lists are wonderful for:

- clarifying thoughts
- identifying patterns or problems
- brainstorming solutions
- getting below the surface
- getting past the obvious
- gathering a lot of information very quickly
- focusing attention on what's *really* going on (*hint:* it's usually *not* what you think!)

There's a catch, though. Make your journal list L-O-O-O-O-O-O-O-O-N-G . . . as in 100 entries! (That's right . . . *100!*)

You can write Lists of 100 on nearly any topic you can imagine. Some suggested Lists of 100:

LISTS

- 100 Things I Need or Want to Do
- 100 Fears
- 100 Things I Like About Myself
- 100 Things I'm Feeling Stressed About

Your list of Lists of 100 can go on forever. (At the end of this chapter, you'll find a List of 100 Things to Write a List of 100 About.) Anything, anything at all, is an appropriate topic for a List of 100, as we shall see.

TIPS FOR LISTS OF 100

Are you thinking you couldn't possibly come up with 100 items for a list on *any* subject? Keep reading. Because here are some tried-and-true tips for journal list making:

- It's OK to repeat!
- Write as *fast* as you can!
- You *don't* have to write in complete sentences!
- It's OK to repeat! (See above.)
- Your entries do *not* have to make sense!
- Just *get it down!*

Let's go over these tips in a little more detail:

• It's OK to repeat. In fact, repetition is a very valid, important part of the List of 100 process. Think of repetition as the telegraph keys of your subconscious mind, tapping away, giving you messages in not-so-secret code.

• Write as fast as you can. Once you get warmed up on your list, it's likely that ideas and thoughts will tumble into

125

your mind faster than you can get them down. Writing as fast as you can allows you to capture the essence of the thought and move along to the next one.

- **You don't have to write in complete sentences.** Use ditto marks, single words, phrases, your own form of abbreviations, or speedwriting. No one is grading your penmanship or grammar here!

- **It's OK to repeat.** I can't overemphasize how important repetition is to the List of 100 process. Write down the very next thing in your mind, even if you've already written it many times.

- **Your entries do not have to make sense.** Every now and then you'll have a random thought that doesn't seem to be connected at all with the subject of your list. Write it down and keep going, no matter how bizarre or far afield a particular entry may seem. Assume your subconscious mind knows what it's doing.

- **Just get it down!** Don't worry about whether or not you're doing it "right." Just do it.

(By the way, don't be concerned that you'll be spending the rest of the day and part of tomorrow writing a List of 100. If you're allowing yourself to repeat and writing the next thing in your mind, you can get through a List of 100 in 20 to 30 minutes!)

LISTS OF 100: A CASE STUDY

Let me give you an example of how a List of 100 can work to give you invaluable information about your inner process.

Beverly had owned her own catering company for about a year. She was facing the usual start-up challenges of tight cash flow, finding new clients, hiring and training good employees, and maintaining her mental health and self-esteem during the stressful, critical time of building her fledgling business.

She told me that she was paralyzed with fear that her savings wouldn't hold out long enough to really get her business off the ground. As we talked, she referred constantly to her fear of running out of money.

Sensing that the money problems were an overlay to a deeper, more fundamental fear, I invited Beverly to write a list called "100 Fears I Am Having Right Now." She wrote the first dozen or so entries rather tentatively. As she warmed up, she wrote firmly and quickly. Her list was completed in 22 minutes.

We then reviewed the list together, looking for "themes." The first theme we found was, indeed, "Money." These were marked with a "$" in the margin:

$ I'll run out of money
$ My business won't make money
$ I won't have enough money to pay the employees
$ I'll mismanage the money I do have
$ I won't be able to pay the bills

And so on.

There were other themes, as well. Another had to do with "paperwork," such as taxes, bookkeeping, and invoices. These were marked with a "P":

P   Quarterly income tax forms are due
P   Accounting/bookkeeping in general
P   I don't know where I put the tax receipts
P   I'm behind on invoices

Et cetera.

And another category, or theme, we called "Failure" and marked with an "F":

F   I'm not making the right decisions
F   My business will fail
F   I won't market my business properly
F   I'll let down everyone who believed in me
F   I'm out of my league

And all the others.

Then we added up all the "$"s and "P"s and "F"s and the other categories we found, too.

And guess what?

Yes, 25 percent of Beverly's immediate fears were around money. (Now you know the *real* reason for a List of 100—it falls so nicely into percentages!) *But 40 percent of her fears were around failure!* And when she took a hard look at that, it made perfect sense to her.

After all, what are money problems if not an external manifestation of a fear of either success or failure? Money, in and of itself, is a neutral commodity. It's just a way of keeping score. Beverly's fear of failure was blocking her from making money, and conversely, not making money was feeding her sense of failure.

The List of 100 Fears indicated very clearly that it was the underlying *fear of failure* that was most important to work with. Money problems were merely a *symptom,* as muscle aches are a symptom of influenza.

The information you can glean from writing the list and breaking it into categories can be richly insightful. If you've received the information or clarity you wanted, it may be appropriate to end the process at this point. But you may want to continue with another journal process that will help integrate and clarify the data you have received. Let your common sense and intuition guide you.

In Beverly's case, having uncovered an underlying fear of failure, it was appropriate to take the process one step further. She divided a sheet of paper in half vertically. She headed the left-hand section "Fear of Failure," and the right-hand section "Reality." Then she took each fear of failure and wrote it on the left-hand side of the page. Across from it, she wrote an accurate statement about the fear. It looked like this:

FEAR OF FAILURE	REALITY
I'm not making the right decisions.	So far, most of my decisions have worked.
My business will fail.	I haven't gone under yet!
I won't market my business properly.	Word-of-mouth referrals are picking up; Yellow Pages ad is working well.
I'll let down everyone who believed in me.	This is ridiculous! I'm not in business to please anyone else!
I'm out of my league.	I am competent, talented, and can hold my own with any other small caterer in town!

By the time this exercise was complete, she had an interesting comparison and contrast between her perceived fear and the truth, and the inevitable conclusion she drew was that she already had whatever it was she was afraid of not having. This "reality check" so delighted her that she left our session furiously jotting ideas for business expansion, new markets, and venture capital.

The next time I saw Beverly, she proudly displayed another

List of 100 that she had encased in a clear plastic protector and carried in her briefcase. This one was entitled "100 Truths About My Business" and included items like "The truth about my business is that I've never had a complaint from a customer" and "The truth about my business is that I charge a fair price for extraordinary service."

"I'm not out of the woods, by any means," she reported, "and money is still tight. But I know I'm going to make it!" Fear of failure had been nipped in the bud—thanks to the List of 100!

ADDITIONAL POINTS

Here are some additional points on Lists of 100:

• **Do remember to number your entries!** Otherwise, how will you know when to quit? Some people find it easiest to number their paper to 100 before they actually begin writing. Others number as they go.

• **Write the list in one sitting.** (It really does take less than half an hour.) It is the sheer volume of entries that dredges up information from your subconscious mind.

• **Generally, a List of 100 has three parts:** The first third usually contains information that you're holding in your conscious mind; your first 30 or so entries might include some repetition, but you'll likely not find any surprises. The second third is often characterized by repetition and the development of "themes" or categories. The last third is where your subconscious mind will have a field day. You'll not only notice more repetition, but you'll frequently surprise yourself with the information on your list. Write it all down, no matter how strange it seems.

In fact, a little bonus of Lists of 100 is that there is frequently a "zinger" somewhere in the last third, usually somewhere in the 80s and 90s. It's very common to have an entry or two that appears to be straight out of left field. (In the example above, Beverly—who was 35, childless, and happily single—amazed herself when she wrote "Having a baby" as fear number 82!)

• After you have completed the list, review it with an eye toward themes. Most lists will group themselves into four to six categories, with Miscellany a handy catch-all for those entries that don't fit anywhere. Mark each entry with its appropriate category. You can do this in the margin by assigning each category a symbol, or you can color-code your categories with highlighter pens. Then go back through and add up the entries for each category. If you have 100 entries on your list, you automatically have the percentage.

• There may be either actual or journal action suggested by the information you have gathered. In a List of "100 Things I'm Feeling Stressed About," I found that 34 percent of my immediate stresses involved my procrastination on filing and clerical tasks in my home office. I immediately sat down and spent three hours catching up on correspondence, filing, and other postponed jobs. Instantly, one-third of my reasons for feeling stressed were removed!

Your list information may suggest a further exploration in the journal that will be helpful. Dialogues and Unsent Letters are frequently useful follow-up techniques. Let your imagination and common sense be your guide.

• Don't overlook the practicality of Lists of 100 as time- and task-management tools. When I found myself in emotional, financial, and legal chaos after my husband's sudden death, an attorney friend helped me create a "to do" list of legal and financial decisions to make, actions to take, and problems to solve. As it happened, the list had exactly 100 items on it. (Unfortunately, there were no repeats!) The prospect of tackling such a mountain of complexity frightened and overwhelmed me. But my friend helped me put it in perspective. "Do just one thing a day," he said, "and the worst will be over in three months." (I did, and it was.)

• Anything that is a current issue for you is a good candidate for a List of 100.

• When you are writing a list of fears, don't be surprised if many of your fears seem nonsensical or irrational. You may, in fact, notice sets of polarities or extremes—with one entry reading, "My boyfriend will want to leave me," and the next entry, "My boyfriend will want to marry me." Or "I'll eat until I reach 300 pounds" and "I'll become anorectic and starve myself to death." When you allow yourself to acknowledge these polarities, you've taken the first step in getting them back into balance.

PROCESS LISTS

As useful as the List of 100 is, its construction allows no room for processing thoughts and feelings until after the list-making is completed. And so there may be times when you write a list, not so much for the information you can gather but for the exploration into your inner state that such reflection allows. The following process list was written by Maggie, who was sexually abused from the age of seven by an adolescent neighbor. It is a poignant example of what Progoff calls "savoring the richness and staring straight into the pain":

Things I Miss

My mom. I need a hug from her. I cried about her yesterday, really sobbed in grief. Death. I still believe that I'll see her again, that she's not gone at all. I realized yesterday that I'll *never* touch her or smell her or hear her or see her on this plane again. I'm too young to have my mother die. God, I miss her.

Kenneth. I miss his tenderness. I miss the unconditional acceptance. I miss the security. I miss the clarity and the truth. I miss feeling so connected with someone. I feel alone. I want him here.

I miss my dad. I want to be near him. I want to crawl on his lap and suck my thumb and be comforted. What if he dies soon? I get scared that I'm losing time with him when I'm so far away.

My dog. I cried about her yesterday, too. I never cried when she died 10 years ago. I felt overwhelming sadness about the loss of her as I cried. She is still one of my greatest friends.

My old house. I can't stand it. I never thought it would belong to someone else. It *was* my mom and dad! I can't deal with the thought of not having that house to come home to. I miss the house more than anything because its loss symbolizes so much.

I miss my grandma. When I see her now, she doesn't know me, or herself for that matter. I won't ever know her as "my" grandma again. She's not that person anymore. I wish I knew when she changed over so that I could have said good-bye.

I miss high school. Insane thought, but I do.

I miss the summer mornings. I miss sitting out on the front stoop with my Captain Crunch cereal watching my mother on her knees in the garden. I miss her obnoxious polyester shorts and tank tops. I miss the grass wet beneath my toes. I miss the cartoons and the consistent ritual of going from friend's house to friend's house, knowing full well that no one was up yet except me.

I miss the dirt. We were always covered with dirt and tree sap. I loved that. There was never a thought of caution about it. We rolled and sculpted ourselves in that dirt. It defined those of us who dared to discover.

I miss breaking my mom's windows by accident, burning down trees by accident, leaving all of the hammers outside overnight by accident, breaking my sister's records by accident, cheating in Monopoly . . . by accident.

I miss the countless times of sexual favors in hot, steamy summer evenings—hidden. I miss the beating, the bleeding, the swelling, the screaming. I miss walking through the neighborhood without a shirt until I was ten. I miss smoking the cigarettes and drinking at eight. The dirty magazines. The stolen money. I miss watching them spray my dog with Raid and stone her. I miss getting it myself after saving her. I miss my mom's constant yelling and criticism. I miss it all because if I could go back I would do something about it. No, I wouldn't.

I miss the honesty. I miss who I was, who I *really* am. I miss the aggressiveness with life, with people, with illusion, with truth. I *knew* then. I knew and I lived in my truth.

100 Things to Write a List of 100 About

1. 100 Things I'm Grateful For
2. 100 Ways I Could Nurture Myself
3. 100 Ways I Beat Myself Up (Sabotage Myself)

4. 100 Things I'm Good At
5. 100 Things I Like About Myself
6. 100 Ways to Be a Butterfly [thanks to Patricia S. McFadden]
7. 100 Blessings
8. 100 Things I've Accomplished in My Life
9. 100 Things I'm Feeling Stressed About
10. 100 Things I'd Do If I Had Time
11. 100 Things I Need or Want to Do
12. 100 Things I Want to Accomplish in the Next X Months
13. 100 Things I Want to Do Before I Die
14. 100 Things That Are Going Right
15. 100 Things That Are Going Wrong
16. 100 Reasons I Want to Stay Married/Committed
17. 100 Reasons I Don't Want to Stay Married/Committed
18. 100 Things I Want in a Partner/Relationship
19. 100 Things I Have to Offer to a Partner/Relationship
20. 100 Fears I Am Having Right Now
21. 100 Things That Once Scared Me but Don't Anymore
22. 100 Things I've Never Mourned or Grieved
23. 100 Things I Miss
24. 100 Sacrifices I Have Made
25. 100 Marketing Ideas for My Business
26. 100 Ways I Can Make Money
27. 100 Talents
28. 100 Jobs/Careers I'd Like to Have
29. 100 Fears About Being a Multimillionaire [thanks to Bob Trask]
30. 100 Things I Believe In
31. 100 Achievements (Qualities) I Am Proud Of
32. 100 Things I Value in Life
33. 100 Ways I Help Others
34. 100 Things That Turn Me On

35. 100 Things That Turn Me Off
36. 100 Judgments I Make
37. 100 Things I Find Hard to Share
38. 100 Things I'm Disappointed About
39. 100 Things I'm Angry About
40. 100 Things I'm Sad About
41. 100 Things [People, Places] I Love
42. 100 Things to Do When I'm Depressed
43. 100 Things to Do When I'm Alone
44. 100 Rules I Have Broken
45. 100 Skills I Have
46. 100 Feelings I Am Having Right Now
47. 100 Childhood Memories
48. 100 Things My Parents Used to Say to Me
49. 100 Ways in Which I Am Generous
50. 100 Fantasies Not Suitable for Polite Company
51. 100 Things I Hate
52. 100 Things I Want
53. 100 Places I'd Like to Visit
54. 100 Things I'd Like Someone to Tell Me
55. 100 Things I'd Like to Hear
56. 100 Things I'd Like to Tell My Child
57. 100 Things I Want My Child to Know About Me
58. 100 Reasons to Have a Baby
59. 100 Reasons Not to Have a Baby
60. 100 Adjectives Describing Myself
61. 100 Decisions Others Have Made for Me
62. 100 Decisions I Made That Turned Out Well
63. 100 Things I'd Do If I Had Six Months to Live
64. 100 Expectations Others Have of Me
65. 100 Expectations I Have of Myself
66. 100 Judgments I Haven't Released
67. 100 Places to Hide
68. 100 Things I Could Carry in My Pocket

69. 100 Things I'd Save If My House Were on Fire
70. 100 Things I Want to Tell My Mother [Father]
71. 100 Things I'd Never Tell My Mother [Father]
72. 100 Financial Fears
73. 100 Excuses I Make for Myself
74. 100 Things I Need/Want to Control
75. 100 Fears I Have About Giving Up Control
76. 100 Answered Prayers
77. 100 People I'd Like to Meet
78. 100 Reasons Why I Get Jealous
79. 100 Things That Make Me Feel Sensuous
80. 100 Ways I Could Safely Be Sensuous
81. 100 Memories from My Past
82. 100 Things That Nourish Me
83. 100 Things I Haven't Finished
84. 100 Things I'm Glad I've Done
85. 100 Things I'll Never Do Again
86. 100 Ways to Generate Income
87. 100 Principles to Live By
88. 100 People I Want to Forgive
89. 100 People I Want to Forgive Me
90. 100 Things to Forgive Myself For
91. 100 Mistakes I Have Made
92. 100 Lessons I Have Learned
93. 100 Past Lives
94. 100 Things That Make Me Cry
95. 100 Things That Make Me Laugh
96. 100 Things I'd Delegate
97. 100 Things I Want for My Birthday
98. 100 Possessions I'm Tired of Owning
99. 100 Responsibilities I'd Like to Avoid
100. 100 Things to Write a List of 100 About

13

STREAM OF

CONSCIOUSNESS

I like Stream of Consciousness because I don't have to think. I get lots more information when my mind doesn't try to figure it all out.

—student of Journaling As a
Therapeutic Tool

As a literary form, Stream of Consciousness writing (also called automatic writing or free-intuitive writing) was popularized by the surrealists in the 1920s and 1930s and by James Joyce in his published works. (Joyce's book *Ulysses* contains several passages of Stream of Consciousness writing, one of which goes on for 72 pages!) As a therapeutic form, Sigmund Freud popularized a sort of verbal Stream of Consciousness with his free-associative psychoanalytic technique.

The purpose of either written or verbal Stream of Consciousness is to invite the subconscious and unconscious minds to empty their purses on a table before you so that you may sift through and see what has been forgotten, what has been overlooked, what can be discarded. It is surely one of the most intuitive journal techniques available.

With Stream of Consciousness writing, you merely begin. With a word, phrase, snatch of song lyric, dream character, or symbol—you begin anywhere at all. If there is something "hooking" you (making you angry, getting your attention), begin with that. Otherwise, just pick something. You may want to experiment with Stream of Consciousness writing by starting with the process of writing itself, as Chrisanne did:

> Writing flows. The written word. Expression of being. Flow of consciousness. The pen seems to move of its own volition. Too fast to think or analyze. Movement, motion, being. One with. Sense and nonsense together. Okay. Amen. So be it. Nothing. All.

MEDITATIVE WRITING

Already you can get a sense of the meditative quality, the slowing down, that Chrisanne derives from her Stream of Consciousness entry. Indeed, one of the values of Stream of Consciousness is its ability to bring you to a state of inner serenity and balance. Chrisanne continues:

> Playing, I like this playing. Words coming words going. One thing and then another. Moments of silence and the roar of a waterfall. The dog barks. The firecrackers explode. My head explodes in joy. My heart saddens in aloneness. All there. Only the cat is quiet. Peaks and valleys. Self/not Self. Calling and calling again and again. Suddenly, quietly, answers from the voice reverberate off the tenuous membrane of being—rocking the walls which

give and bend and flow and still remain. Songs unsung—
beauty unseen. All is there and real and can be touched
gently—so gently.

OVERCOMING OBSTACLES

Another benefit of Stream of Consciousness writing is its ability
to show you the barriers you perceive in a given situation, and
perhaps some routes over, around, or through the barriers, as
Lily's entry illustrates. She began with an image of herself in a
very high building, looking out of a window into fog:

> Blank, nothing, fog, confused, confused, confused, not
> knowing, frustrated, nothingness, held back, a wall, high
> wall, thick wall, brick wall, no doorway, hidden, treasure,
> bright, shiny, valuable, quiet, serene, joyous, flying,
> high, free, soaring, love, happiness, complete, gossamer,
> fragile, precious. To go on: life, beauty, newness, birth,
> infant, hope, joy, love, marriage, home, comfort, warmth,
> nourishment, servicing, receptive. . . .

"I'm sure this entry started out as a picture of the unknown
before me," remarked Lily, who was eagerly awaiting word on
an overseas job. "I feel like my destiny is in someone else's hands
while I wait to hear. Yet there *is* a doorway, even if it's hidden,
and just look what's on the other side! It makes the waiting
easier."

You can use Stream of Consciousness in a similar way. When
you find yourself confronted with a seemingly insurmountable
barrier, let your imagination float freely around, over, and
through it. This can be a very effective warm-up technique for
a Dialogue with a block or resistance.

ACCESSING JOY AND CREATIVITY

Because Stream of Consciousness writing emerges so spontaneously, there is often a sense of childlike joy and wonder at the images offered up:

> Rainbows dancing unicorns prancing I'm so high I touch the sky can't come down I'll break my crown and then I'd cry and cry and cry don't stop yet the poem's not done since I'm so high I'll touch the sun. . . .

The same sense of freedom and rhythm can loosen the grips on creativity and allow a rich flow of images. Poetry is often the result!

FLOW WRITING AND IMAGERY

A variation on Stream of Consciousness writing is called flow writing, where you begin with an image and follow it wherever it leads:

> I see myself in a long, dark, and incredibly lonely tunnel. Yes, I am lonely! I am very lonely! I want to turn and run, but there is nowhere to run. The tunnel extends forever in both directions. No light. I feel stifled. It's hard to breathe in this tunnel. Is it time to quit yet? No. What am I avoiding by being in this tunnel?
>
> Avoidance is a void dance; I pirouette in blackness, hoping for nothing, receiving the same. . . . It seems to me that the answer is to not think, not act, not relate, not respond. Be in the blankness and the blackness. Be in the tunnel. . . .

A thirty-minute flow-writing session three or more times a week is an excellent discipline for meditators and creative writers. The images often build on one another, and so in a couple of weeks you'll have something resembling a short story. The story's plot, of course, is your own inner journey. Fascinating!

METAPHORIC FLOW WRITING

When you begin seeking metaphor and synchronicity in your life, you'll find it, and Stream of Consciousness or flow writing is an excellent vehicle through which your intuitive knowledge of meaning and purpose can speak to you. As symbols reveal themselves to you, try flow writing about them, as Laura did in a piece she calls "Vernal Equinox":

> This afternoon, five weeks after I met you and one week after you became too important to me, I saw a ragged old donkey in the big field behind the waterfront motel. She was tied to a tree, and I thought she was waiting for me to come play with her. And so I did. I patted her dusty head and let her gum my hand. She bumped me, nuzzling me again, and I forgot that anyone in the world existed but us two.
>
> A long rope anchored her to the tree and was coiled several times around the trunk so she couldn't reach her water or her oats. I pulled her gently to me to free her, trying to help her meet her needs, but she didn't like that at all, and she grew suddenly wild, wrapping the rope around my legs as well. She knocked me down hard and would have kicked me but that I rolled away.
>
> Some man came then and chastised me for bothering the donkey, and he said never to pull the rope because she

would kick me even though she seemed gentle and eager to play. And he told me to go away because I would only cause trouble and there might be legal problems after all.

Feeling foolish and a little lost, I walked slowly away to the street and across to the bay where I saw the spring equinox moon rising full and as golden round as a Spanish doubloon against the twilight. And looking at it, I remembered you and me, and I thought of how that ragged old donkey was a perfect metaphor for my fantasy of loving a man who is not free.

TIPS FOR GETTING STARTED

• **Begin with an entrance meditation.** (You'll find two of them at the end of this chapter). If you're doing a Guided Imagery, ask a friend to (slowly!) read the castle meditation aloud. Or you can read the meditation into a tape recorder.

• **Be patient with yourself.** You won't necessarily get wonderful, insightful, inspiring results the first few times you try this technique. Don't give up on it too soon.

• **Try writing with your nondominant hand.** This seems to occupy your left brain with the task of concentrating on motor skill and thus frees up your intuitive side.

• **Write in circles, chunks, or angles.** Varying the "top to bottom, left to right" style of your writing is an invitation to intuition.

• **Begin with nondirected drawing or coloring.** Start with "flow art" and let the writing emerge.

• **Commit to writing for a predetermined time period.**
You'll usually get somewhere if you stay with it for 30 minutes.

ENTRANCE MEDITATION:
STREAM OF CONSCIOUSNESS

Let yourself relax.
Become very comfortable in your body, and close your eyes.
Take a slow, deep breath . . .
    hold it . . . and release it.
    Do it again . . .
    and again.
And now imagine that you are looking out of a window.
Notice the view.
And now imagine that there is a rolled-up window shade at the top of the window
    and you are now reaching up . . .
    and very slowly . . .
    beginning to pull the window shade down.
As the window shade crosses your line of sight . . .
    you see that it is completely white . . .
    and soon you are looking at
    a completely . . .
    blank . . .
    screen.
And as you look at this blank screen . . .
    allow your mind to empty itself of thoughts.
    No thoughts . . .
    no thing . . .
    allow yourself to think of no thing . . .
    nothing at all.

Stay there, quietly emptying your mind of thoughts . . .
  stay there for as long as you please . . .
  and when you open your eyes to write,
  you can begin with any word or image that suggests itself to
    you . . .
  following the thread of that word or image . . .
  letting it guide and direct you.
And for now, just watch the white screen.
When you are ready,
  open your eyes,
  take a deep breath,
  and begin to write.

ENTRANCE MEDITATION:
GUIDED IMAGERY

Adapt this castle imagery to fit your favorite fantasies. The key
ingredients: a journey, a destination, a message, one or two
places to explore, an obstacle, a gift, an encounter with a person
or animal. . . .

Take a deep breath and relax.
Allow yourself to become very comfortable in your body, and
  close your eyes.
And as you breathe deeply,
  imagine that you are on a journey.
  Only you know the purpose of this journey. . . .
  Allow yourself to know that purpose now.
As you travel on your journey,
  you see up ahead, far in the distance
  a castle.

You are weary and ready for rest.
You travel toward the castle.
And now you approach the castle.
As you do, you notice the castle gates.
There is a scroll attached to the gate . . .
a scroll with your name on it . . .
a very special message just for you.
And so you read the scroll,
taking its message into your heart.
You pass through the gates,
through the castle gardens,
noticing as you do
a place on the grounds
to which you will return.
Now you are at the main door of the castle.
You walk inside . . .
look around . . .
noticing the sights and smells and sounds of the castle.
And now you transport yourself
to a room of the castle . . .
a room with a closed door
that opens as you approach it.
Enter this room . . .
notice the sights and smells and sounds. . . .
In this room there is a gift for you.
Discover this gift now. . . .
Let its meaning make itself known to you.
Stay in this room as long as you please. . . .
And when you are ready,
you can return to the castle grounds
and begin to move toward the place you have already chosen
to visit.

STREAM OF CONSCIOUSNESS

As you approach this place
    you encounter an obstacle. . . .
    allow yourself to overcome this obstacle.
Now you are at your chosen place.
Take a moment to rest . . .
    to think about your destination . . .
    your message . . .
    your gift. . . .
    Sit and refresh yourself.
When you are ready to continue on your journey,
    you walk back to the castle gates,
    and there waiting for you
    is a friend . . .
    perhaps a human friend,
    or an animal friend,
    or a spirit friend.
This friend bids you godspeed
    and whispers in your ear
    a message of wisdom for your journey.
And so, taking with you your message . . .
    your gift . . .
    the memory of the obstacle . . .
    and your words of wisdom . . .
    you continue on your journey.
When you are ready,
    open your eyes,
    take a deep breath,
    and draw or write about your journey.

14

STEPPINGSTONES

The Steppingstones are indicators that enable a person to recognize the deeper-than-conscious goals toward which the movement of his life is trying to take him.

–Dr. Ira Progoff
At a Journal Workshop

The Steppingstones technique is one of the most significant contributions that Dr. Progoff's Intensive Journal™ workshop makes to journal therapy. "When we speak of the Steppingstones of our life, we are referring to those events that come to our minds when we spontaneously reflect on the course that our life has taken from its beginning to the present moment," Progoff writes. "The Steppingstones are the significant points of movement along the road of an individual's life."

Let's imagine that you're hiking in the mountains. Your trail ends at a shallow stream and then picks up again on the other side. You and your hiking companions decide that crossing the stream is no problem; you'll just step on the stones, one at a time, until you're across and on the other side.

If you think of the stream as the whole, ongoing movement of your life, how did you get from where you were to where you are? Which stones did you select? Probably some were flat and large, and you felt secure. Others might have been pointed, teetery, or deceptively slippery. These may have been the Steppingstones you wanted to move away from quickly, because they didn't feel as safe. But they were more exciting!

And so the Steppingstones of your life are the markers, the places you paused, the times when perhaps you said to yourself, "Ah, my life will never be the same again." Progoff emphasizes that the Steppingstones are neutral "with respect to pleasure or pain, progress or failure. They are simply the markings that are significant to us as we reconstruct the movement of our life."

This is an important point to keep in mind. Go back to the metaphor of the stream. As far as the stones are concerned, you could be a small child skipping playfully. You could have just slipped and cracked your head. The white water could be up, and you could be pulled by the current. Or you could be trout fishing, for all the stones care. The stones are completely neutral; they are unmoved by any emotional significance you may attach to the event. The stones are just the stones.

It is important to remember this when you are listing your Steppingstones, because it is common to review your list and say, "Oh my, this is too depressing. I need to lighten up a little and think of something happy!" Conversely, you may look at your Steppingstones, all of which elicit positive feelings, and say, "This is shallow and without depth. I'd better put in a tragedy or two." To the extent that you possibly can, allow each Steppingstone to present itself to you as its own gift, without regard for the ones that come before or after.

Limit your selection of Steppingstones to about 12 or 15. The intention here is to select those life events which seem to have had significance within the context of *how you are living your life today*. Out of all the hundreds of thousands of experiences you have had from birth until this moment, let only a dozen or so come into foreground. These are the Steppingstones of your life *as you are perceiving it at this moment.* It is important to realize that if you were to write a Steppingstones list once a month for the next year, you probably wouldn't have two that were exactly the same. That is because the life events that affect your life *as you are living it today* will change as your life circumstances change.

LISTING THE STEPPINGSTONES

Progoff recommends that the first Steppingstone on your list be, "I was born." This simple opening statement acknowledges your physical, emotional, and spiritual birth into your body, your family, your culture, your society, your world.

You may then choose to list your significant life markers chronologically, or they may come to you in random order. It doesn't matter. It is helpful, though, to put them in chronological order after you are through with your list so that you may sense the underlying rhythm of your life. Without knowing anything else about Nancy, we can begin to sense the drama and hardship of her life:

1. I was born
2. My father left
3. My mother died
4. My father returned
5. I left home to get married
6. I had my daughter
7. I had my son
8. I raised my kids

9. My husband left
10. I followed my heart
11. My husband wants to come back
12. I am being reborn

You may write Steppingstones lists from any number of different perspectives. Nancy's is a wide-angled list that covers all the territory of her life.

Nancy could also write the Steppingstones lists of any or all of the four *functions* of which we are made up: body, mind, heart, and spirit. (Jungian typology refers to these elements as the sensate, thinking, feeling, and intuitive functions.) When Steppingstones for each of the four functions are substituted for Nancy's wide-angle list, we get the impact of a zoom lens:

Feeling (Heart)

1. I was born
2. I felt loved and taken care of
3. I felt insecure and unloved when Daddy left
4. I felt loved and needed
5. I felt devastated and broken when Mother died
6. I felt distrustful and wary
7. I felt loved and wanted
8. I felt loved and needed
9. I felt needed
10. I felt used and thrown away
11. I began to love my life again
12. I feel torn and confused
13. I feel confident that I will know what to do

Thinking (Mind)

1. I was born
2. At three, I learned the word "responsible"

3. I was second-grade class monitor
4. I tried to run the household after Mom died
5. Dad and I fought a lot
6. I married Bill
7. I had Marcy
8. I had Stu
9. I studied a lot on my own while I raised kids
10. Bill decided I wasn't good enough for him because I'd stayed home and raised kids instead of being a career woman!!!
11. I started college at the age of 38
12. Bill seems to think we should try again
13. I don't know what I want

Intuitive (Spirit)

1. I was born
2. I loved freely as a child
3. My innocence died
4. I turned to my spirit friends for comfort
5. My mother's spirit visited me in dreams
6. My father and I clashed
7. I left home
8. I had out-of-body experiences in childbirth
9. I started going to church
10. I quit going to church
11. The kids and I practiced mind reading
12. Bill dumped a load of garbage on my intuition
13. I trusted my heart's desire
14. It is leading me places I've never been

Sensate (Body)

1. I was born
2. I learned to swim

3. I reached puberty
4. I felt fat
5. I gained and lost 20 pounds
6. I had a baby
7. I lost 40 pounds
8. I had another baby
9. I lost 60 pounds
10. I gained and lost 35 pounds
11. I took up aerobics
12. I gained 20 pounds
13. I wondered if I would ever have a real relationship with my body

Can you begin to see the themes develop and take shape? When the Steppingstones are broken down in this way, new and rich dimensions begin to take form.

WRITING ABOUT THE STEPPINGSTONES

As you review your list, it may seem that you have written a seemingly random series of events. Upon closer look you will realize that each Steppingstone on your list is a microcosm of an entire section of your life. Contained in the short phrase you have written are memories that may span several years.

Writing about the entire time frame suggested by the Steppingstone allows you to recapture the events and moments that shaped your destiny. And as you recall the time, you will often find that lessons left incomplete are offered back up for learning, old wounds that never quite healed are offered back up for healing.

The phrase, "It was a time when . . ." is the Springboard from which we can enter each of the Steppingstone periods:

- It was a time when loving hearts and arms welcomed me to the world.
- It was a time of fascination.
- It was a time when crashing thunderbolts of Fate brought me to my knees in pain.
- It was a time of knowing my connection with the ancient healing wisdom of the desert.
- It was a time of ripening.

As you contemplate the metaphor or emotion that completes the phrase "It was a time when . . . ," allow yourself to turn not only your thoughts but also your feelings, your body, and your very soul to that period in your life. You may experience a rush of memories, images, associations, even smells and tastes. Savor this rush. Allow yourself to wash in it. And then when you are ready, quietly and in stillness, begin to write about the Steppingstone period:

It was a time when life was exquisitely painful, a loose tooth which hurts divinely when wiggled. And Kathi and I wiggled the loose tooth of life with abandon, that summer of 1966.

We didn't know quite how to define ourselves; we only knew we were "deep." Stranded in a time warp between the beatniks and the hippies, we had no language for our questions, no larynx for our cause. It was a fine time to be fifteen, to embrace Life, with all its pain, and seek the Truth.

Our heroine was a playwright's Luisa, who cried out our impassioned prayer: "Please, God, please, don't let me be *normal!*" Like Luisa, we knew our superior destiny; we knew we were special. We solemnly reinforced this in each other, gazing endlessly with vast respect into each other's souls, nodding sagely and smiling wanly and expecting that any minute, Life would announce itself to us, and we would wordlessly surrender.

I think of it now, and the image that comes to mind is a squinching up of the face, a wriggling like a wet cocker spaniel puppy, an excitement that every pore of the body would experience that which there was to behold—made more provocative by the knowledge that we had no idea what that entailed.

It was all a lovely mystery, set to a nonstop background melody of Rod McKuen and Ferlinghetti poetry. We ached for the chance to experience heartbreak; we longed for a love we could lose. We wrote haiku and free verse that summer, wrote it endlessly. Poetry tumbled out of us like chaff against the grain, ever flowing, a spontaneous fountain of syllables chronicling our loving, our crying, our hurting, our never knowing why. But we knew, because Gibran told us, that there could be no pleasure without pain, no laughter without tears, no joy without sorrow. And so we wept until we had no tears to weep and our laughter through the tears turned from hilarity to hysteria, and when there was no more breath to laugh, we cried again. That summer of 1966 was an endless cycle of loving, living, wanting, giving, and always with the supreme, sublime knowledge that *someday* . . .

. . . it would all make sense.

OTHER APPLICATIONS FOR STEPPINGSTONES

Progoff recommends that you write the Steppingstones for your Dialogue partner as preparation for entering the Dialogue relationship. Continue to write in the first person and begin with "I was born," just as you would your own Steppingstone list. If your Dialogue partner is inanimate, think of the "I was born" step as the birth of the situation, energy, complication, illness in your life. It may seem awkward or difficult to write the Steppingstones for another, because you may feel you don't have enough information. Let your intuition guide you, and write down what you do know, filling in with what *might* have been. Writing the Steppingstones for another can be a very revealing process!

Generally speaking, Steppingstones lists are comprised of short phrases or sentences. But particularly when you are working with the Steppingstones of a relationship, consider writing the Steppingstones in prose, allowing each turning point in the relationship to tell its own little story.

Try exploring your Steppingstones in art. Color and shape offer rich and evocative dimensions to the Steppingstones. Title each picture with the Steppingstone period and the completed phrase, "It was a time when. . . ."

ENTRANCE MEDITATION

Allow yourself to relax.
Close your eyes.
Take a slow, deep breath . . .
   hold it . . . and release it.
   Do it again . . .
   and again.
And now begin to imagine
   that you are sitting in a theater.
   And on the screen . . .
     . . . is the movie of your life.
Watch the images go by . . .

. . . the images of the turning points of your life as you are living it today.

Feel the rhythm and flow of your life events.

From birth to the present moment . . .
notice how your life has unfolded.
Notice the events at which you can say,
"Ah, my life was never the same again after that particular decision or event."
These are the Steppingstones of your life.

There's no need to do anything . . .
but watch . . .
and feel . . .
and notice.

Stay there as long as you please.

And when you are ready,
open your eyes,
take a deep breath,
and list the Steppingstones of your life.

15

TIME CAPSULE

The Time Capsule technique is like the old Jim Croce song. But instead of saving time in a bottle, I get to save time in a book.

—Write On! workshop participant

We've talked about how the journal can be a valuable tool to help you stay aware of your life as it unfolds over the long term. Perhaps by now you're beginning to develop a sense of how your journal can serve as a valuable aid in helping you pinpoint your own unique cycles, patterns, and rhythms.

It is a fact of journal writing that the journal tells its story over time. When you have been writing regularly for several months or years, you'll discover that much of the pleasure and value comes from the assimilation of information and data that is recorded when a series of days, weeks, and months intertwine into an intricate and beautiful tapestry.

The Time Capsule is a versatile tool that reviews the activities of your life and structures them into a cohesive story. A time capsule in a cornerstone contains the essence of society at a particular point in history; a Time Capsule in journal writing captures the essence of your life as it was being lived at a given moment. Time Capsule entries are periodic logs written on a daily, weekly, monthly, quarterly, even yearly basis.

DAILY TIME CAPSULE

There's a lot to be said for the one-year diaries we used as children. Consider buying one for your daily use. They are readily available in greeting card, stationery, or drug stores; they fit neatly into a purse, tote bag, or briefcase. For maximum privacy, they still even come with locks and keys!

Use this small format to record a summary of each day. You'll find that space will prevent writing more than about 100 words, which can be both a blessing and a curse! But you'll quickly develop the knack of capsulizing your daily activities, highlights, moods, and achievements in a few well-chosen sentences.

These brief entries will often tend to focus on the *content* of your life as opposed to the feelings generated by the content, which can more appropriately be explored in longer journal sessions. But you'll learn through a daily Time Capsule that it isn't always necessary to cathart or write at length to gain value and pleasure from the journal. Even 100-word summaries of daily experience can weave the fabric of your life.

Your daily entries—however mundane they may seem, taken individually—will evolve into the punctuation marks of your life. And even sporadic entries can contain precious nuggets of memory for the future. Christine tells of finding her mother's diary, years after her death:

> I remember giving Mother this diary for Christmas in 1976. Inside, Mother had dutifully written only on the six lines appointed to each day. She began the day my father died of cancer:
>
> **March 14** Ralph very bad today. Died 10 p.m. after having a severe chill. . . . Went to mortuary for arrangements.
> **March 18** The funeral was held at 2 p.m. Craig held my hand during the service. A very cold day. . . .
> **March 19** Weather abated a little. Christine and children came to see me before they left. . . .

Christine continues:

> Mother died six weeks later. She had written only a few other entries in her diary. Why she had thought to include that Craig held her hand during the services is a mystery to me. My son was five years old then, sweet, innocent, and sensitive. Perhaps it was his presence of unconditional love that touched Mother's heart that day. Today, at seventeen, Craig does not remember that day, or his grandfather or grandmother. But his sensitivity of that day had been recorded by his grandmother, and because of that innocent strength, that childlike love, that comfort, his small token of love will be cherished forever.

MONTHLY TIME CAPSULE

Another excellent application of the Time Capsule technique is recording your life's activities and events on a monthly basis. Blank bound books are an especially appropriate format for monthly logging, as one volume will contain several years of entries. There's something wonderfully satisfying about going to your bookshelf and taking out a single book into which is chronicled a five-year anthology of your life, one month at a time!

You'll have the best results if you plan to spend at least an hour on your monthly Time Capsule. The actual writing probably won't take that long, but you'll want to allow sufficient time for reflecting on your month.

Begin by gathering together the memory joggers you'll use to reconstruct your month. These can include:

- your daily diary, if you keep one
- your longer journal entries
- your checkbook. How you spent money can remind you of how you spent time and energy. A check to your favorite clothing store might remind you that this month was a time of creating a new image for yourself; a check to a bookstore might help you recall that you began a new course of study
- your business or personal appointment book, again to help you focus on how and with whom you spent time

After you have refreshed your memory on the inner and outer workings of the month, sit back and relax. Use the entrance meditation at the end of this chapter, or devise one that will work for you.

It doesn't take long to reap the benefits of this technique. For many people, rhythms and cycles begin to appear after only three or four months of regular Time Capsuling.

Monthly Time Capsule entries are most effective when they are written regularly. Therefore, if this technique appeals to you, commit to it for six months. You can then review your entries and decide whether it is something you'd like to continue.

ANNUAL TIME CAPSULE

Esquire magazine's January cover is always devoted to the Annual Dubious Distinction Awards. *People* magazine reserves its year-end issue for the 25 Most Intriguing People of the Year. *Life* magazine presents The Year in Pictures. You, too, can keep a personal history of each year through your annual Time Capsule entries.

December is a great month to make note of what worked and what didn't. Many a journaler spends a delightful winter afternoon creating a jigsaw puzzle of memories of the year just past.

Try a list of your favorite things: movies, books, television shows, songs, moments, people, celebrations, surprises, lessons, quotations, classes, achievements, experiences, and whatever else is important to you!

Or write a list of Best Things/Worst Things for the year. As I was writing my December 1985 Time Capsule entry, I became aware that it was a year I was ready to have behind me. It seemed as if the lessons had been hard, the victories sporadic. Yet I sensed that I might be shortchanging some of the year's good times. So I titled one page in my Time Capsule book "Best of 1985," and on the opposite page I wrote "Worst of 1985." And then I let loose with my recollections.

Under both lists I wrote, as fast as I could think of them, the people, places, things, events, circumstances, experiences, and memories that came to mind as either "best" or "worst." I filled up those two pages with no problem, continued with "Still More . . ." titles on the following pages, and kept going. Near the bottom of the second page I found I was winding down with "worsts," but the "bests" were still going strong. The "bests" ended up outnumbering the "worsts" by about 25 percent, and reading over the lists never fails to bring a chuckle, a shudder, a smile.

Another variation on the theme: write a list of "100 Successes, Accomplishments, Achievements, and Completed Goals" for the year just past. It's wonderfully validating to review the year in terms of your successes, and it's a nice perspective from which to begin goal setting for the upcoming year.

Here's the simplest, easiest Annual Time Capsule of all: Tear out the "highlights of the year" article from the late December newspaper and file it in your journal!

TRAVEL TIME CAPSULES

Whether you travel for business or pleasure, don't leave home without your journal.

Marta, a schoolteacher who travels every summer, types out the highlights of her vacation log upon her return home. She mounts these excerpts next to the appropriate photographs in a scrapbook for a permanent show-and-tell story of her travels. Because some of her trips qualify for teacher recertification credit, her journal does double duty by serving as documentation of the educational activities she pursued.

Business travelers find a daily log invaluable for notes on people they met with, outcomes of meetings, memory-joggers of follow-up activities, details of contracts and agreements, and financial records for IRS and expense reimbursement purposes. And trip reports can be created easily from the journal notes.

Some tips for travel journals:

- **Keep a memo-size spiral-bound notebook in your purse or pocket.** Jot notes to yourself as you go through your day—a fascinating bit of local lore shared by a tour guide, the charming bistro where you stopped for lunch, the friendly shopkeeper, the delightful bed-and-breakfast with the great bathtub.

• **Set aside thirty minutes each evening to review your day in the journal.** Your notes will jog your memory and enable you to summarize your daily activities and discoveries.

• **If you're on a whirlwind tour, keep a separate page in the front or back of your journal for the barest of outlines.** Because vacations will often throw you into a strange sort of time warp—especially if you're spending only a day or two in each location—entries such as the following will prove very useful when your traveling companion says, "Is it Friday already? Where were we on Wednesday?":

> **Monday, June 15** Arrived London. Figured out the Tube. Checked into Harlingsford Hotel. Saw *Mystery of Edwin Drood*.
> **Tuesday, June 16** Sightseeing—Tower of London, Westminster Abbey, St. Paul's. Saw *Starlight Express*.
> **Wednesday, June 17** Rented car, left for southern coast. Lunch in Brighton. Stayed at B&B outside Portsmouth.

• **Check out the preprinted travel journals available at many stationery stores.** If you like structure and simplicity, these books are just the thing. Similar to one-year diaries, these books are lightweight, small enough to slip into the side of a tote bag or backpack, and have spaces to record items of travel interest, such as the weather, the mileage, souvenirs purchased.

• **Take advantage of postcards.** If photography is not your forte, picture postcards of your travels make wonderful illustrations for your journal! Write your daily log directly on them.

ENTRANCE MEDITATION

Find a comfortable position, and close your eyes.
  Take a slow, deep breath . . .
  hold it . . . and release it.
  Do it again . . .
  and again.
Now gently turn your thoughts to the past month.
Notice the emotional, or feeling, tone
  that you first link with this period of time. . . .
Now, holding that feeling tone, begin to reflect
  on the events and activities of the month.
  Notice the awarenesses you came to . . .
  the lessons that you learned . . .
  the people who were important to you in this month.
Become aware of how you spent your money . . .
  your time . . .
  your energy . . .
  your other resources.
Allow your thoughts to drift . . .
  freely and comfortably . . .
  across this month-long time span
  for a few moments.
If there are other feelings that come to you,
  become aware of them.
And now allow a word or phrase to come into your mind,
  a word or phrase that best describes the month as a whole.
Keeping that word or phrase in mind
  to help you focus,
    supplement it with your recollections and feelings about this
      time frame.

Stay there as long as you'd like . . .
   and when you are ready,
   open your eyes,
   take a deep breath,
   and begin to write a Time Capsule for the month just passed.

16

TOPICS DU JOUR

16 Topics is the best-kept secret of business success!
—Write to the Top workshop participant

Topics du Jour is a journal technique that allows you to start moving mountains, one boulder at a time. Originally designed to meet the needs of business executives who were "too busy to stay on top of everything," Topics du Jour allows you to keep an ongoing chronicle of your life at monthly intervals.

31 TOPICS: MONITOR EACH AREA OF YOUR LIFE

The concept is simplicity personified: Number down a page from 1 to 31. Write in each space *one* area of your personal or professional life that you would like to monitor. Then, each day, look at the topic that corresponds in number to *today's date*. If today is the 25th of the month, find number 25 on your list. What's the Topic du Jour? Use it as a Springboard.

So far, so good. Not significantly different from other journal approaches. But just wait. Next month, on the 25th, you'll be writing about the same topic you wrote about today! Now you can begin to chart the process of change in your life.

31 TOPICS IN ACTION

Here's how it looks. These examples come from the journals of Rusty, a single mother.

Rusty's 31 Topics

1.	Rituals	16.	Money
2.	James [boyfriend]	17.	Counseling
3.	My job	18.	New relationships
4.	Spiritual life	19.	Dreams
5.	Journal writing	20.	The world around me
6.	Old friends	21.	Successes
7.	PMS	22.	Community service
8.	Habits	23.	Lessons
9.	Projects in planning stages	24.	Synchronicities
10.	Body/health	25.	Things to improve
11.	Blessings	26.	School
12.	Parents/family	27.	Monica [daughter]
13.	Goofing off	28.	Upcoming events
14.	Selling house	29.	Completions
15.	Frustrations	30.	Reflections
		31.	Looking ahead

May 2. James. He's busy; I'm busy. Haven't had much quality time together. We leave lots of notes and talk on the phone at least twice a day. In a way, it's nice to have this time of supplemental communication. I hope it doesn't last much longer, though. I miss him.

May 7. PMS. Tired a lot, even when I get plenty of sleep. Might be iron deficiency. My period was extremely heavy this month, and I had a couple of terrible PMS days when I felt like I sincerely could have killed someone. Pity the man who would try to rape me or hurt Monica while I'm having a bad PMS day. I think, under the right combination of circumstances, that I am capable of murder. That's a terrifying thought.

► ACTION STEP: Take iron supplements.

May 25. Things to improve. Discipline in getting up. Exercise program. Stop worrying about money. Organization. Simplify. Do more journaling. Be less cluttered. Eat better food. See James more often. Spend more time with Monica. Stop worrying about insurance.

► ACTION STEPS: Cut down on red meat.

Call insurance agent.

June 2. James. We seem to be in a very pleasant space. Spending more time together now, but not as much as we usually do. There's a consistently higher quality to our "alone" time. He's invited Monica on a fishing trip when school is out. She's thrilled. So am I—a whole weekend to myself!

June 7. PMS. Better this month but still not good. This is the third difficult month in a row. Time to check in with Dr. Stevens. Iron supplements seem to be helping; I'm not as dragged out.

► ACTION STEPS: Make gyn. appt.

Continue with iron suppl.

June 25. **Things to improve.** Clutter. Junk food. Plan for Monica's summer.

> ◗ ACTION STEPS: Call about summer camp.
> Schedule a yard sale.
> Quit eating red meat!!!!

Note the use of Action Steps to highlight things to do, people to contact, etc. Review the prior month's entry before you begin to see if there are any unfinished Action Steps to carry forward.

Although it doesn't matter in what order you place your topics, hold an awareness of your individual monthly rhythm when you create your list, as Rusty did with the PMS topic. Many journalers like to put "money" or "budget" near the date(s) corresponding to payday. The 30th of the month is a nice time for a look back or a look ahead. The 1st is a good date for monthly goal-setting. Include "Successes" at least once on your 31 Topics list!

Conveniently enough, the seven months with 31 days are spaced evenly throughout the year, so #31 is a good slot to reserve for reviewing and updating your list.

Most office-supply stores carry expanding file folders with pockets numbered 1 to 31. Clip your 31 Topics list to the outside of the folder and drop each day's entry into its date slot. You'll have immediate access of prior entries for Action Step and general review.

16 TOPICS: BIWEEKLY BUSINESS CHECKUPS

For business purposes, you may want to adapt this technique slightly and call it 16 Topics. Begin in the same way, by numbering a page from 1 to 31. Monitor biweekly instead of monthly by repeating your topics every 15 days:

TOPICS DU JOUR

16 Topics

1.	Cash flow	16.	Cash flow
2.	Marketing	17.	Marketing
3.	Accounts payable	18.	Accounts payable
4.	Accounts receivable	19.	Accounts receivable
5.	Advertising	20.	Advertising
6.	Successes	21.	Successes
7.	Etc.	22.	Etc.
. . .		. . .	
15.	Two-week plan	30.	Two-week plan
	31.	Business review	

A 16 Topics journal can be maintained in less than 15 minutes a day and, over time, evolves into a valuable business history for any number of purposes—taxes, marketing, administrative, or personnel. Not incidentally, an ongoing 16 Topics journal also holds your personal career history—very helpful for creating résumés!

Reserving number 15 and number 30 for a "two-week plan" gives you the opportunity to highlight the upcoming time frame. The months with 31 days are good occasions for an overall business or project review.

No wonder Kevin, a banking executive, calls 16 Topics "the best-kept secret of business success!"

17

UNSENT LETTERS

[Unsent Letters] are like an emotional enema. They move the crap right out of you.

**—student of Journaling As a
Therapeutic Tool**

Unsent Letters are marvelous tools for the "three C's"— catharsis, completion, and clarity. One of the most popular and widely used of journal techniques, Unsent Letters are wonderful for expressing deep emotion, such as anger or grief. They are also tools of choice for gaining closure and insight. And they are an effective way of communicating your opinions, deepest feelings, hostilities, resentments, affections, or controversial points of view in a safe, nonthreatening atmosphere.

The trick to an Unsent Letter, of course, is: *don't plan to send it!* This gives you the permission to write without censorship, risk, or fear of hurting someone else. Of course, you may decide at a later time that you want to share what you've written. If you do, you are certainly free to do so, but writing it with the knowledge that it is initially for your eyes only allows you to "tell the complete truth faster."

CATHARSIS

Try writing Unsent Letters to the crazy-makers in your life. Let it all out. Use four-letter words. Say the rudest things you can imagine—the things you'd *never* really say to someone. Tell them they're jerks. Tell them why. Tell them what you're going to do in return. Indulge yourself in all the perfect squelches that don't occur to you until after the moment is gone.

Then tear the letter up. Or burn it in the fireplace, flush it down the toilet, rip it apart with your teeth, throw it on the floor and jump up and down on it.

Let yourself holler or grunt while you're doing this. Try screaming at the top of your lungs. Beat your fists into a pillow and give it all you've got. (Forewarn your housemates, and maybe your neighbors!)

Chances are excellent that you'll either feel better fast or collapse into a giggling heap on the floor.

Doug, a real estate developer, came to class irate at a business associate whom he considered responsible for an unsuccessful closing. He fired off an Unsent Letter to her, and his dramatic reading of it to the class burned the ears, blued the air, and would have earned him a role in summer stock. Then he wadded up the letter and ground it into the carpet with his size-14 cordovans—and grinned.

In the next class, he told us this story: The day after he discharged all that frustration and anger in the Unsent Letter, Doug ran into Marilyn, the closer he held responsible for botching his deal. As soon as he saw her, he burst into laughter. She asked him to share the joke, and Doug told her candidly how angry he'd been after the closing, and how he'd gone to journal class and written her a nasty letter.

Marilyn listened in amazement as Doug calmly told her that he was disappointed in her work. So disappointed, in fact, that he was thinking about changing closers. He gave her three or four specific suggestions of ways she could retain his business.

"When I got back to my office," Doug said, smiling, "there were a dozen red roses on my desk! And a note telling me how much she appreciated my honesty in telling her how she could give better service to her clients."

Unsent Letters help you dump extra baggage so that meaningful communication can take place.

Don't fool yourself into thinking that your "negative" emotions aren't real. They are. And allowing for their discharge—in appropriate ways, of course—is a healthy stress-reducer.

COMPLETION

Unsent Letters can also help you come to closure with any relationships that are unfinished. Write to those people in your life who have left you, or whom you have left. Tell them all the things you'd say if you could. Try this with the people who are still in your life, too, if it's time for your relationship to shift gears.

Patricia's life took an unexpected turn when an automobile accident fractured her pelvis and shattered her legs. "As I lay in my hospital bed, I was aware of replaying old tapes about the various relationships in my life," she said. "I began to realize that I am the one who is in charge of how I relate, and I am the one who can effect change in the roles that I play out."

After she left the hospital, Patricia used Unsent Letters to articulate what was going on in her various relationships and release herself from roles that she found limiting. "In some of the relationships, I was looking for a sense of completion; in others, a new perspective from which to relate," she said. She wrote letters to her mother, her deceased father, her sister, a woman friend whose house she was living in rent-free, a former lover, and a man she wanted to date.

"I didn't send any of the letters," Patricia said. "But I felt the effects on every one of the relationships. My emotional channels are cleared for the first time in years. It feels wonderful."

Particularly when a relationship has ended by death, Unsent Letters are a gentle way to keep your loved one alive in your heart while allowing the healthy grief process to take its natural course, as it did for Rebecca, a graduate student. Each month, Rebecca received a letter from her grandmother with a check enclosed. And each month she would promptly write back, expressing appreciation for the financial support and catching her grandmother up on her activities.

"When my grandmother died of a stroke," Rebecca reported, "I dealt with two losses: the very real grief for my grandmother, whom I loved very much, and the loss of my financial stability. I was afraid I'd confuse the two—'My grandmother died, and now she can't help support me financially.' So I continue to write letters to her each month, but now I write them in my journal. I tell her how much I miss her, how I'm doing in school, what's going on in my life. I'm also using the Unsent Letters to explore the dynamics of grief and loss. It's very healing."

CLARITY

Unlike a Dialogue, an Unsent Letter is a *one-way* communication. It is an opportunity to express without interruption or discussion. Such expression can result in air clearing and a deeper sense of clarity about your own position.

In Pamela's Unsent Letter to her college-aged daughter, she reflected on her own feelings of inadequacy as a mother:

> How I wish I had a chance to start over, to raise you again. You were my biggest challenge, my greatest fear. . . . I was afraid of you, afraid of not doing the right things. Divorcing your father helped ease the tension, but still I didn't know how to raise you. I would have separated earlier, but I was afraid I couldn't handle you alone. If only I knew then what I am learning now—to listen, to value you, not to battle. If only I could do it over, raise you with more patience, more understanding, more consistency, more positive support, more of my time, more of me. . . . Now you're almost an adult. And you do seem more at peace; the anger is gone. I am happy for that. I love you more than you can know.

"Even though I started out writing this letter for my daughter, it quickly shifted into a letter I was writing for myself," Pamela commented. "As I relived those years of struggling and unhappiness, I realized I didn't always know who was raising whom. I did the best job I could. I can't undo the past, but I can certainly bring my new awareness and knowledge to the present and future."

In an unpublished paper, Bill tells of a technique used in marriage and relationship counseling called the "Love Letter":

> This technique allows you to move through all five levels of feeling: anger/blame; hurt/sadness; fear/insecurity; guilt/responsibility; and love/understanding/forgiveness. These feelings will never make sense unless they are each given a voice so that the incoherent feelings can be cleared out.

The letter begins with anger and blame, the part of you that feels you're right and your partner is wrong. ("You're so mean, you selfish jerk.") It's not a time to intellectualize, but to let it all hang out. The next step is to identify feelings of hurt or sadness related to your partner. ("I felt devastated when you didn't say good-bye before you left on your trip. I feel so hurt.")

After expressing the hurt, you will begin to feel some fear and insecurity that needs to be shared. ("I'm afraid you'll leave me forever.") Also, the insecurities of any unknowns or distrust can be shared at this time. ("When you left without saying good-bye, I was afraid you might have an affair while you're gone.") The next step is to share guilt and take responsibility for your own actions. ("I'm sorry I wasn't more direct in asking for what I wanted. I feel guilty that I yelled at you.")

After you have expressed the other four levels of feeling, you will begin to feel a deep emotional connection with your partner. Love, understanding, and forgiveness will naturally emerge. ("I love you very much. I know you're probably feeling as rotten as I am about the way we fought before you left. But we'll get through this. Thanks for hanging in there with me!")

Surprisingly, the purpose of the letter isn't to communicate to your partner how you're feeling. You're writing this for yourself, to help you resolve your own feelings and to get down to your own love.

"SENT" LETTERS

Although the art of letter writing has waned as high tech has waxed, do develop the habit of keeping copies of the letters you write to relatives, friends, and other correspondents. Lloyd, a grass-roots environmentalist, keeps a notebook of letters he sends to the editors of local and national publications. "It's an anthology of my changing positions on the current events of our lives," he remarked. "These letters represent some of the highlights of our nation's progress and relapse in environmental concerns."

Years ago, I was in a long-distance relationship with a career military officer; our letters flew halfway around the world at the rate of two or three a week. When we agreed to discontinue our correspondence, he graciously returned to me two shoeboxes stuffed with my letters. (I, of course, had an equal number of his!) I now have four notebooks filled with an ongoing, three-year exchange of our inner and outer events, philosophical musings, relationship clarifications, and individual growth. It's a piece of my personal history.

TIPS FOR WRITING UNSENT LETTERS

• **Don't censor; don't edit.** Allow yourself to get it out. This may feel uncomfortable, especially if you are dealing with rage. Remember that this energy isn't going anywhere of its own accord; if you don't get it out of your system, it will lurk around in your body, heart, and mind. Do you really want that much anger undischarged?

• **Unsent Letters don't hurt anyone.** Many people fear that giving voice to their ugliest feelings, even in the privacy of an Unsent Letter, will bleed through to the target of their anger or pain. Assuming that you are using the Unsent Letter as a discharge of your own feelings rather than as an attack on someone else, this will not happen. Consider destroying the letter after it is written, not only to protect yourself and the subject of your letter, but also to symbolize the release of the "negative" feelings.

• **Your Unsent Letter may be to anyone or anything.** It is perfectly valid to write a letter to someone who is no longer living or who has not been born yet, to an organization or institution (the Communist party, the Catholic church) that is not realistically an audience, to a part of yourself, or to a famous figure to whom you do not have access.

• **Start your letter with a Springboard.** "What I've been most afraid to tell you is . . ." or "I want you to know how I feel about . . ." are effective openers. So are "[expletives deleted]"!

• **Write a letter *to* yourself *from* someone else.** This can give you an entirely different perspective, with resultant insight. Imagine the possibilities!

• **Letters to and from God are magical!** Alice Walker's Pulitzer Prize–winning book, *The Color Purple,* is an entire collection of Unsent Letters to God. Start your own collection!

18

PERSPECTIVES

The Perspectives technique takes me to different times and places. It offers insights that I might not have seen. It helps me get unstuck.

—student of Journaling As a Therapeutic Tool

Perspectives is a journal technique that allows you to explore the possibilities of the roads not taken in your life. With Perspectives, you can step into the future or the past, resolve interpersonal differences with compassion, and glimpse the world as it might have been for you—or as it might be for another. It is a process of altering your personal reality, your world view, to try on another perspective.

DECISION MAKING

Perspectives can be a valuable tool in the decision-making process. When you find yourself up against a life choice—a career change, a move to another part of the country, a turning point in a relationship—you can gain valuable insight by using Perspectives to fast-forward yourself in time and space and write from the point of view of having already made the choice.

One day Beth got a sudden itch to move to California. She didn't know why she felt drawn to head west; she just knew it was time for a move. Although both San Francisco and San Diego appealed to her, she hadn't spent enough time in either city to make an intellectual choice.

"I knew this was a strictly intuitive move I was making," Beth reported. "There was no rational reason to move, and there was no rational way to make the choice. Something inside of me was at work here. I knew my intuition would guide me to the right city."

Beth's intuition found a voice when she used Perspectives to help clarify the choice. She wrote two journal entries, each from the perspective of having been in the new city for three days. This is how each one read:

> **San Francisco.** It's cold, it's rainy, it's foggy. Apartments are ridiculously expensive and I haven't seen anything I like. I've run into some unfriendly people. I'm lonely and I want to go home. . . .
> **San Diego.** The bougainvillea are blooming, it's 75 degrees, the sky is gloriously blue. I've found a really neat house close to the beach, and I have an interview with an art gallery tomorrow. I love it here!

Beth moved to San Diego and, at last report, was living in a "really neat" house close to the beach and working in an art gallery!

Not every Perspectives entry you use for decision making will have a prophetic quality to it, but it's an excellent vehicle to give your subconscious mind a voice as to what it is holding as an *expectation*. Whether or not the weather would have been foggy and cold on Beth's third day in San Francisco is anybody's guess, but this process allowed her to bring forward her *attitude* that San Francisco might be a cold, foggy, unfriendly place. And since our subconscious expectations exert a not-so-subtle influence on our conscious perceptions, life becomes a self-fulfilling prophecy. If Beth had been looking for unfriendly people, she undoubtedly would have found some!

We often block ourselves from really knowing what we want because we think we can't have it or we shouldn't want it. But we hold in our awareness, even if it is on the unconscious level, an inherent wisdom that wants to guide us in the direction of our fullest development. The Perspectives technique can give this wisdom a voice.

UNDERSTANDING OTHERS

A proverb attributed to Native Americans, "Never judge a man until you have walked in his moccasins," suggests another excellent application of the Perspectives technique. A journal entry written as if you were someone else provides the opportunity to step into another person's skin long enough to sense what might be going on for him or her. The compassion afforded by this discovery makes it an invaluable tool for healing yourself and your relationships.

Katherine, who was having extreme difficulty accepting her parents' divorce after 30 years of apparently happy marriage, ran across a formal portrait of her mother taken on the dual occasion of her parents' engagement and her mother's 21st birthday.

Drawn by the pensive expression on her mother's face, she wrote as if she were her mother sitting for her portrait:

Autumn, 1957. I am sitting, poised for the camera to go off. I feel anxious. I hope I look calm.

It is a time of big change in my life—I am turning 21, coming of age, and I have just become officially engaged to Martin.

I thought I would be feeling so happy, so elated. This is something I have been waiting for—both turning 21 and being officially engaged. We have known for a while we would be getting married—and now, the time is now. It's official.

It feels so final.

What have I decided for myself in marrying Martin? What path am I turning around? I meant to write "turning down." Do I feel like I am going around in circles? Do I want to *turn around* and go back to being unengaged and living, working, and enjoying myself in New York?

Am I making the right decision? Is Martin the right man for me? Am I the right woman for him? There are times when things feel so right and good between us—and there are times when I begin to feel the emptiness, the space. But those are just my fears. Silly fears.

I wish the camera would go off. The wait feels interminable.

Something doesn't feel right, but it's too late to back out. Is it too late? Am I too late to feel my feelings?

Hurry up. I want to move. I've got to get going so I can make plans for the wedding.

Click.

Thank goodness.

Katherine's journal entry concluded with newfound compassion:

So much going on for you even then, Mom. Why couldn't you listen to yourself? You've held so much back. And you knew all along, didn't you? Dad claims he did, too. Yet neither one of you could back out. I guess you weren't meant to—until 30 years later. I thank you for not backing out. If you had, I wouldn't have been born. But I'm sorry you were so unhappy. I'm sorry you couldn't have shared your unhappiness with someone. I hope you can find happiness now. I truly do. And I want you to know I'll listen to you. You don't have to hide behind the calm exterior anymore. I'll be your friend.

GLIMPSES OF THE FUTURE

The Perspectives technique can also hurtle you forward in time, allowing you to create a visionary picture of what you want your life to be like. This can be a very important factor in aligning your will with your unconscious desire, thus helping to "create your own reality."

To do this, merely begin your journal entry with a date sometime in the future. Then, in an entrance meditation, focus on that date. What will your life be like on that date in the future? Which of the problematic situations in your life today will no longer be hanging around? What new roads have you traveled? What choices have you made? How have you grown?

Try writing a "One Year from Today" entry on your birthday each year. Put it away and forget about it. On your next birthday, review it. You might just be amazed at how prophetically it speaks to your accomplishments over the last 12 months!

Jean, whose cross-state residential move triggered a long-stored grief process (see chapter 20), found solace in a Perspectives entry that she wrote two weeks prior to the actual move.

Her page was dated six weeks in advance, as if she had been living in the new city a month. This entry gave her a glimpse into the future and anchored in her mind the fact that she wouldn't be living in chaos forever:

> It is June 1 and I've been living here for about a month now. I'm not completely settled, but I think I'm going to like it here. I love being able to walk to school and ride my bike to work. My cat seems to be adjusting well, too. . . . This is home for me now. It's warm, it's comfortable, and I can have friends over. It's bright and sunny and I have enough room to move around. . . . I take walks in my new neighborhood, I speak to my neighbors, I sit and enjoy my backyard. . . . The hard part is over. The furniture fits, the phone is installed, the plants survived the move. My energy is present, my smells are here, my possessions surround me. The transition has officially taken place, and my spirit will catch up soon. Rome wasn't built in a day, and my lessons in patience will probably never be over. But it feels okay. When I open the door, the place looks familiar. . . .

As a bonus, this Perspectives entry provided Jean with some very direct instructions on ways she could make the settling-in process easier for herself. In the first 30 days, she was careful to invite friends over, take walks in her new neighborhood, speak to the neighbors, burn incense and candles right away so that her "smells" would be present, and place her best-loved objects in view of the front door.

ROADS NOT TAKEN

The Perspectives technique can also allow you to explore, with hindsight, the roads you chose not to take. Robert Frost's poem

"The Road Not Taken" eloquently captures the inherent paradox in living: every choice *for* contains within it all of the choices *not for*. A choice to marry is a choice not to stay single. It is also a choice not to marry any of the other persons whom you may have married.

If you find yourself haunted by "what if?"s or "if only"s, go back in your journal to the situation you did *not* choose. Pretend you chose it, and write about how your life would be today.

Marie left her executive job to go to graduate school in a completely new career field. Two years later, she felt inexorable pangs of nostalgia about the life she had left behind. The desire to ask for her old job back (even though it had been filled by someone who was doing an outstanding job) tugged insistently at her. She wrote from the perspective of having stayed at the company:

> I've just been promoted to senior vice president, which was more title than salary. Starting an evening M.B.A. program next month. If I can get through the accounting classes, I'll probably do fine. I'm responsible for new product development now—guess I always was, but now I can't say "it's not my job" when it doesn't get done. Life is good. I'm meeting some interesting men on my travels, but since they're clients, my love life is only great in my fantasies. I feel like I'm at a place where I want to start entertaining. Intimate little dinner parties for eight. Maybe I'll take a gourmet cooking class. . . .

"There is no question in my mind. That is exactly what my life would be like today if I'd stayed," Marie reported. "Would I trade? No way. I can't imagine surviving an M.B.A. program. I wouldn't trade my lover (whom I wouldn't have met if I'd stayed) and our quiet life-style for a hundred charming men in exotic cities. And an intimate gourmet dinner for eight? Give me a break! We round up everybody who answers their phone and throw salmon on the grill."

If you use this technique to explore roads not taken in situations where you weren't necessarily the one doing the choosing, proceed with caution. It may be more painful than productive to focus on what life would have been like if your father hadn't died when you were four—*unless* you are willing to let him be alive in your awareness. Megan uses what she knows about her father, together with how she imagines he would have been, to create an intimate relationship with the daddy she never knew:

> Daddy's 57th birthday. We surprised him with cake and candles at the golf course. He'd never met the other people in his foursome before, but they joined right in as if they were old friends. Everybody's an old friend around Daddy. . . . As I do every year, I told him what I'd learned from him this year. Today I said the gift he had given me this year was the gift of finding joy in the smallest, most unexpected places. I've needed that so very much this year, with the divorce and all. . . .

ENTRANCE MEDITATION (ONE YEAR FROM TODAY)

Take a moment to become comfortable in your body.
Relax . . . close your eyes . . .
    and take a slow, deep breath . . .
    hold it . . . and release it.
Do it again . . .
    and again. . . .
And as you breathe deeply and relax,
    imagine that there is a calendar before you . . .
    and you are looking at today's date.

Now imagine that this calendar is for the next year . . .
   12 months . . .
   52 weeks . . .
   365 days from now. . . .
And in your imagination,
   begin to turn the pages forward . . .
   until you reach today's date once again.
It is one year from today.
And now begin to place yourself in space and time
   one year from today. . . .
Begin to imagine yourself as you are one year from now.
You are one year older. . . .
And as you review the year just past
   you can stop to take note . . .
   of the journey you traveled.
You can recall the most enjoyable parts of the year . . .
   the challenging spots . . .
   the lessons you learned.
And as you review the year just past . . .
   you notice how you are today.
   where you live . . .
   how you live . . .
   the work you do . . .
   the challenges ahead . . .
   the opportunities in view . . .
   the parts of your life that make it joyful. . . .
Stay there as long as you like. . . .
When you are ready . . .
   Open your eyes,
   take a deep breath,
   and date your page one year from today.

19

DREAMS AND

IMAGERY

Why not wake to each new day as a new adventure in life, sometimes difficult and sometimes flowing? And why not wake to the day excited and committed to capturing The Dream, that product of the night? To waste the dream in forgetfulness is to waste a third of our lives, perhaps the most creative third at that.

—Strephon Kaplan-Williams
The Jungian-Senoi Dreamwork Manual

Dreams and mental images are like newspapers. When they are fresh and timely, they provide invaluable information about our inner world, just as the morning paper tells us all we care to know about the outer world. Yet, like newspapers, there's always a fresh one tomorrow, and yesterday's dream or image, if left "unread," quickly loses its flavor.

Most therapists who work with dreams routinely request a dream log from their clients. This dream journal is brought into the counseling session, and it is not at all uncommon to spend an entire session on one dream. In fact, it's not uncommon to spend an entire session on one dream and not be complete with it!

Common sense tells us, then, that even if you were in dream therapy weekly, you wouldn't be able to unlock all of the information available in your dreams unless you did some "homework." With a little practice and the generosity of your journal, however, you can learn to work with your own dreams and gain precious insight into the workings of your unconscious mind.

Some therapists—and Dr. Progoff's Intensive Journal™ system—recommend that your dreams be recorded separately from any other journaling you are doing. Whether dreams are separated out or merged in with other entries is, like so many other aspects of creative journal writing, a matter of both personal preference and an educated consideration of the pros and cons of each.

Perhaps the biggest advantage of keeping your dreams in a separate section of your journal, or in a separate journal altogether, is that you'll have a running "script" of your dream life. Reading through dreams sequentially can provide a fascinating foray into the warp and weft of your unconscious. Just as your chronological journal points out the cycles, patterns, and themes in your "outer" life, so will your dreams reflect the cycles, patterns, and themes of your "inner" life—albeit with a great deal more subtlety.

When the personal process journal and the dream log are combined, however, the sum of the parts can create a greater whole. Reading a dream separate from its context can be akin to watching a foreign movie without the subtitles: the action may be fascinating, but without a reference point the interpretation can be awfully subjective.

And so the primary advantage to keeping your dreams filed right in there with your other entries is that when the "inner" life is reviewed within the context of the "outer" life, meaning is offered to each. "And it is this interrelationship," writes Tristine Rainer in *The New Diary,* "that a natural, chronological diary makes apparent." She continues:

> The added benefit is that the night dream and the day life remain complementary sides of an integrated being. You can tap the emotional energy and intuitive wisdom of a dream when it first delivers its message. In retrospect, you can see even more patterns and interconnections, and you can also observe to what extent you successfully listened to and answered your dreams in your waking life.

WHY WORK WITH DREAMS?

A dream is a gift from your unconscious mind—creative, imaginative, with plot twists that rival any soap opera. And you can have private screenings every night of your life, at absolutely no charge!

It's amazing how transparent your life can become when you learn to tune in to these miracles of the night. In the scope of this brief exploration of dreams and the journal, I cannot even begin to do justice to the rich and evocative study of dream psychology and symbology. I would refer you instead to the many fine books published on the subject, some of which you will find listed at the back of this book.

Suffice to say, then, that your dreams serve purposes both profound and mundane. Some dreams function as a sort of inner secretary, reminding you of tasks left uncompleted or real-life events that may have slipped your conscious mind. (My "dream secretary" reminds me of dental appointments by providing me with a dream of having a tooth filled the night before I'm scheduled for a checkup!)

Other dreams can point you down a path of inner awareness

and growth. Still others can help clarify difficulties, relationships, parts of yourself that are clamoring for attention. And sometimes dreams can lead to life-changing decisions.

In his book *Dreams: Discovering Your Inner Teacher,* noted pastor and Jungian psychotherapist Clyde Reid tells of such a life-changing dream, although he is quick to point out that it was his *response* to the dream, rather than the dream itself, that caused his life to take a completely different turn.

As a young man, Dr. Reid had been hired for a coveted position as a college administrator. "But then I had the dream," he says, "the dream that changed everything."

> I dreamed that Jesus appeared alongside me and said, "Are you ready to come and help me?" I replied, "Yes, I think I am."
>
> I had never paid attention to dreams before that. I had no idea that dreams were important. . . . But I knew this dream had grabbed me and would not let me go. I kept asking people whom I respected what they thought it meant. And then I didn't want to hear their answers. I was on my way as a college administrator, and I didn't want any interference. So I began my new job, and I loved it. It was everything I had hoped for. But I kept wondering about that dream. Finally, about nine months later, I resigned my new position and went off to study theology to see if there was anything in it.
>
> I have never regretted my change of career. I know it was what I was intended to do with my life, and had I ignored it, my energies and direction would have gone sour.

"We dream to wake to life," Strephon Kaplan-Williams states simply. Dreams are, indeed, a celebration of life.

HOW TO INCREASE DREAM RECALL

Dreams are also slippery and elusive. How can they best be remembered?

First of all, take solace in the knowledge that dream recall *can be learned.* It may not happen instantly, but persistence pays. Keep trying!

And try any combination of these suggestions, in any order:

• **Keep a notebook, pen, and small flashlight by your bed.** Write at the top of a fresh page: "[Tomorrow's date]— Dream Log." This gives your unconscious mind a clear statement of your intention to record a dream upon awakening.

• **When you awaken with a dream, write it down immediately.** Remembering dreams can be like taking the lid off of a can of vapors: here this instant, gone the next!

• **Disturb your waking environment as little as possible.** Don't get out of bed or turn on a harsh light upon awakening. Try to avoid alarms or clock radios. And try to stay in the same physical position in which you awakened until your dream is recorded.

• **Go to sleep with the conscious intention of remembering your dreams.** As silly as it sounds, try singing a few choruses of "Mr. Sandman, bring me a dream" as you're falling asleep. Or write an Unsent Letter to your Dream Self. Or use Laura's poem to the Dreamkeeper as a benediction to your day (or write your own poem):

Brown Bear, Guardian of Sleep, Keeper of Dreams
Stand beside me in darkness,

Your warm, rich animal scent
Grounding me on the earth plane
While my spirit soars.

In your powerful arms
Catch the mood of my unconscious
Keeping still my demons with your mighty jaws
And hold them there, Brown Bear,
Until jeweled morning light
Opens my eyes.

May the four directions bless us
This night, and to you, and to them,
And to dreaming, I offer burning
Smudge of fresh mountain juniper.
Let us sleep . . . and dream.

• **As you fall asleep, try visualizing yourself writing your dream in your journal.** Or write it on a mental blackboard.

• **Write down *anything* you remember from your sleep,** even if it is a fragment, a scene, a feeling, a mood. The barest snatches of recall can give you something to work with.

• **Especially write down any dream that frightens you, baffles you, seems particularly odd, or from which you awaken with a distinct feeling in your body.**

• **Write what comes to you, in whatever order it comes.** It isn't necessary to reconstruct your dream in chronological order when you're first writing it down. You can always go back and make sense of it later on.

• **Try a hand-held tape recorder by your bed.** (But remember to transcribe the tape later on!) Often, you'll amaze yourself with details you don't recall consciously when you review the tape.

• **Be good-natured about the process.** If at first you don't succeed, keep trying.

WORKING WITH YOUR DREAMS

The beauty of working with dreams is that there are no "right" or "wrong" interpretations. A dream interpretation is "right" if it fits for you. That's all there is to it.

No one can accurately interpret your dream for you. Dream therapists who are trained in symbology, theory, and technique can serve as *valuable guides* to the process. But because we are all magically different, our dreams are uniquely individual.

It is true that some dream symbols tend to have universal, or archetypal, meaning. On the archetypal level, for example, snakes symbolize transformation along the death/rebirth continuum. But the death/rebirth continuum does not always mean physical, mortal birth and death. It can mean psychological, emotional, spiritual, or transpersonal death and rebirth. It can mean the death of one habit and the birth of another. And your individual imprint of the snake symbol can also be influenced by your personal history with snakes. If, as a child, you had a pet garter snake who was your friend, confidant, and ally, your "snake" dreams will be quite differently interpreted from those of someone who was bitten by a rattlesnake as a child and was rushed to a hospital for an antivenin injection.

And so the first guideline is to approach other people's interpretations of your dream and its symbols with a healthy skepticism. You may, of course, happen to agree with their analysis, but only you hold the key. For example, in any bookstore, you can find paperback books that use a dictionary approach to symbols; these can be a handy double check, but for the most part, you're better off with your own intuition and common sense.

The next guideline is to assume that every character, every symbol, every setting in your dream represents a part of you or your current life. This can be taken as a guideline no matter how bizarre or fanciful your dream locales and symbols, no matter whether the characters are familiar to you or straight out of the funny pages. How can a dream about Aunt Myrtle represent a part of you, you say? Start by checking in with what you know about Aunt Myrtle. If Aunt Myrtle is overbearing, smothering, and manipulative, ask yourself, Is there a part of me that is acting overbearing? Or who or what in my life feels like it's trying to smother and manipulate me?

With all of this in mind, you're ready to begin working with your dreams.

LISTS OF TITLES

For starters, get in the habit of giving each of your dreams a name, just as you would title a short story or a movie. A running list of your dream titles is a simple and effective technique that allows the emergence of patterns and themes.

To find the title, review your dream after you have written it down. Then note the most significant symbol, feeling, event, or character. The title will naturally emerge. (If it doesn't, make one up.)

You can then keep a "dream index" by title and date on a separate page in your journal. This way you can not only quickly find specific dreams, but also you'll find that patterns and themes will jump out at you.

Leslie's list of dream titles from a two-month period included these entries: Armaggeddon, My Baby Died, Monsters, My

DREAMS AND IMAGERY

Father Is Dying, XYZ Unrest, Mama's Boy, The XYZ Murders, Death and Destruction, An Autograph for Joe, Joe's Comfort, Joe Goes Camping, Joe and the Darkening Rain, Compassion Without Pain, Pushing Joe's Buttons, Processing Through Joe, Wise Babies, Frank Gives Birth to Twins, Doting Aunt, Twins in the Tunnel. The list of titles alone, even without reading the dreams, gives a clear picture of the death and birth themes that were prevalent during this time period. Leslie explained:

> Specifically, I was processing through the "death" in my life of an important social, spiritual, emotional, and political outlet, the XYZ Foundation. I was about to either quit or be fired from my job with this nonprofit agency. Unknowingly, I was also preparing myself for the end of a significant love affair. This relationship ended after only four months [My Baby Died], when Joe, a married man I was dating, renegotiated with his estranged wife [My Father Is Dying]. After Joe broke up with me, I experienced a flurry of "Joe" dreams, in which my soul healed on a deep level even while I slept. Finally, the *plural* "rebirth" aspects of my dreams [note the two appearances of twins] attested to not only my healing from two major emotional shocks, but also the celebration of new life which I found when I began a wonderful new job and formed a new friendship with a lovely man.

Noting in the journal any overall or specific implications which arise as a result of reflecting on the dreams can offer important insights, as well as bring up other areas to be worked through in the personal process portion of the journal. After the first several dreams, Leslie wrote:

> The death dreams seem to have predicted not only the death of XYZ in my life but also the completion of a lot of other relationships—including, most ironically, Joe.

Perhaps the one about my father [My Father Is Dying] represented my fear of losing something that makes me feel secure and loved. The one about calling Joe and having his mother refuse to put my call through [Mama's Boy] occurred the night before he and Debra left for the weekend trip that precipitated his breakup with me. . . . In my death dreams, I am sometimes serene and accepting [Armaggedon, My Father Is Dying, Death and Destruction] and other times filled with a consuming grief or panic [My Baby Died, Monsters, the XYZ Murders]. This must represent the two levels I am feeling consciously. On one hand I know it is necessary to have a part of it die, or at least be willing to give up my attachment to it, in order for it to be reborn. On another level, though, I'm sad and angry and very frightened that it will evaporate if I let it go.

The journal entries continued with cathartic writing that dealt with Leslie's anger, grief, and fear.

TECHNIQUES TO TRY

Clustering is an excellent way to access your individual associations to symbols or dream characters. Unsent Letters to and from the characters in your dreams can offer insightful information about their relationships to you. Writing a Captured Moment of a scene in the dream—focusing on the sensory details and letting your imagination run free—is a good way to amplify the dream. Drawing the dream characters, symbols, moods, or just colors can be a powerful way to experience a dream's messages from another dimension.

A staccato list of symbols, images, impressions, observations, and questions can point out places to explore. Using the identification technique from Gestalt therapy ("I am the [dream symbol or character], and I . . .") is one of the easiest and most powerful ways to access information about your dream. Active imagination with symbols and characters is a standard dream technique with Jungian therapists; in journal parlance, this is called Dialogue. If all else fails, try Stream of Consciousness, or reenter the dream through imagery and flow-write about it.

When does it all end? It ends when you know it's ready to end, when you run out of time or interest or desire, when you get an "aha!" It's a good idea, no matter how much or how little work you've done on a dream in your journal, to wrap it up with at least a brief entry—perhaps an Unsent Letter to your dream self—highlighting your learnings and synthesizing all of the information you've received.

There is fertile soil to be tilled when dreams and images are approached creatively from the journal standpoint instead of obligingly logged and forgotten. If dreams and images are cryptic answers for our lives, then the journal is a bridge into the mysterious messages of our minds.

SECTION III
PUTTING IT ALL TOGETHER

▼

INTRODUCTION

We baby-boomers are a generation of adult children who are choosing to break the chains of our familial dysfunction. The tasks of working through long-stored grief, healing childhood wounds, and recovering from dysfunctional families of origin are perhaps the most prevalent—and painful—therapeutic issues of the late 20th century.

Estimates place the number of Americans raised in alcoholic households at 28 million, and experts guess that up to 80 percent of the adults in our society were raised in a family which was dysfunctional in some way. In other words, most of us did *not* have a childhood that resembled "Leave It to Beaver," "Make Room for Daddy," or "The Brady Bunch"—three of the many television shows of the genre featuring wise fathers, dimpled mothers, and relentlessly cooperative children.

Instead of the idyllic television families we yearned for, many of us grew up in homes where one or both of our parents were physically or emotionally unavailable to us. Sometimes the disease from which our parents suffered was alcohol addiction. Sometimes it was Valium addiction, food addiction, work addiction, church addiction, or gambling addiction. Sometimes it was addiction to authority and rigidness; sometimes it was addiction to pain and suffering. No matter what the addiction, there was usually a secondary addiction operating in other family members—an addiction to the addict and the dysfunctional life-style. (This secondary addiction is now recognized as an illness in its own right; its name is co-dependence.)

Whatever the particular weakness in our family, we learned at an early age to survive it. Like a wildflower growing out of a rocky ledge, we found magnificently creative ways to adapt to our inconsistent environments. We learned as children how to function and cope as if we were adults.

As children, some of our generation were routinely beaten, sometimes to the point of serious physical injury. Some were sexually abused. Some were made responsible at a heartbreakingly early age for the physical and emotional needs of our families. Some of us tried to parent our parents. Some of us bore up stoically under a ceaseless barrage of criticism, insults, and verbal abuse. Almost all of us were lonely, hurt, and confused, and even though we are now all grown up, that sad and hurting child still lives within. Physically, we are adults; emotionally, many of us are still children.

The chapters in this section deal with some of these painful issues. In chapter 20, Jean Jameson shares her experience with using her journal to process grief. Edelle Kinsinger provides a thoughtful look at healing childhood wounds in chapter 21, and in chapter 22 Cynthia Walser suggests ways that Adult Children of Alcoholics (and other dysfunctional families) can use the journal as a guide to the unfolding of possibilities.

Your journal can serve as steadfast companion and confidant on the troubled and sometimes harrowing journey back to your true Self. You'll find other help stations along the way if you need them; nearly every community has regular meetings of groups such as Al-Anon, Adult Children of Alcoholics, and Co-Dependents Anonymous, which have helped millions whose hearts are wounded.

20

THE FIVE STAGES OF GRIEF AS EXPERIENCED IN MY JOURNAL

by Jean Jameson

You may my glories and my state depose, But not my griefs. Still am I king of those.

–William Shakespeare
King Richard the Second

Every now and then I become aware of how perfectly things fall into place without any effort or control on my part. The springtime of 1987 was one of those times: by some stroke of destiny or fate, I took classes in both journal writing and death while I was moving through the first conscious grief experience of my life. My journal provided the perfect forum to explore the five stages of grief: denial, anger, bargaining, depression, and acceptance.

The event which precipitated my grief might seem as if it wasn't all that shattering. I moved from my mountain home of

12 years to a larger city 150 miles away. I soon became aware, though, that it wasn't just the move that I was dealing with, but all of the grief and loss of my life that had gone untended. A lifetime's worth of grief was triggered by that relocation.

How did I arrive at the decision that grief was a big issue? It wasn't as if I woke up one day and proclaimed: "Yes, I know now what has been bothering me lately. It is my unprocessed grief." Hardly! The awareness unfolded gradually (as awarenesses usually do), through dreams, feelings, internal nudgings. And all of these were first noticeable in my journal:

> **April 5** I am struck by the efforts I have gone to in order to avoid pain, grief, death. Both my own and others. My dog dying. Moving from the only home I'd ever known when my father's business went bankrupt. The bankruptcy, and loss of financial stability. My grandmother's death. The loss of my childhood, my innocence. And so many others. I never got the chance to be complete with these situations, so when I think about them, I'm thrown back into the midst of the pain and grief that I never had a chance to process. So I feel in the thick of that frustration, of being in the grief, and not having the slightest idea of what to do with it. So now I just cry and cry and cry and cry.

> **April 14** . . . As I say that, tears come to my eyes and my sadness wells up from that hidden place right beneath the surface. . . . I have some fears about that. What will it feel like to be present with my feelings of loss? Oh, my heart. . . .

> **April 17** I noticed this evening that I resented the beautiful days and late daylight hours and I wanted it to be dark.

> **April 19** [I recorded a dream entitled *Killing the Wolf*, in

which I was being pursued by wolves who were my grief.]

And so the issue began to have clarity at this point. Thanks to my journal, I knew what I was confronting. At any point in time before I began journaling, I believe I would still be lost in that wasteland, wondering what was wrong with me, without a clue as to what to do or why.

I do not remember being taught anything about grief. On the rare times when I saw my parents or other adults dealing with grief-provoking situations, they did so by denying, evading, or ignoring the issues. Therefore, I thought that pain was something I wasn't supposed to feel, and when I did feel pain, I quickly learned to stifle and suppress it. I learned these lessons well, and I honestly thought I was doing the "right" thing all of those years that I refused to let my grief and pain come to the surface.

However, through those same years has come a gradual unfolding of capabilities and awarenesses that have challenged these limiting concepts I had learned. So the task became not only to challenge the rules I had established, to change some of my core beliefs, but also to acknowledge the existence of deep and painful feelings of grief. I was consciously moving out of the first stage of grief—denial. This denial was not about one specific loss, but rather about the process of grieving, as I expressed in the first of several journal poems:

Do not speak to me of grief
Do not notice how my sadness pervades my being.

That is just the way I am.
My face does not naturally smile.

Leave me alone.

Let me say there is nothing wrong
Let me believe everything is fine.

It is not worth being concerned about.
It is only my raging Soul crying,

"Do not ignore me,
I want to be more."

And at last I said, Yes. Yes, I will look into the darkest depths and see what lies there in torment.

I had not a clue as to how to go about moving out of denial. How did I start looking at something I had refused to believe was there? And suddenly I was angry. I was angry at my lack of ability to live my life on the level I would like. Through it all was the journal. Just as the journal had brought the issue of grief into focus, it was helping me to move through the anger.

April 20 What beliefs have been formed for me through this process of dismissal? When did I get the message that no matter what the request was, the answer was a resounding NO? My world is not ruled by desires and truths but by rules and regulations, and my individuality is unimportant and insignificant. Is this the point at which I begin to retreat—further and further away from all that I am?

A life of have-tos, can't-haves, you-don't-matters; keeping thoughts and feelings hidden away; too sensitive, too vulnerable, too hurtful—stuff it away. What do they want? Figure it out. If you can come up with what they want and fulfill it you will be powerful. You will be in control. Be all they desire and they will desire you—forget you—you whoring bitch who will pay the price to be needed—dependency, addiction, mucky mire of falsehoods and negatives.

April 22 I feel the tightening in my face returning.

April 24 I was aware again the other evening of feelings of resentment about the Springtime.

PUTTING IT ALL TOGETHER

It is at this point that I again praised the virtues of the journal. I had very seldom expressed my anger to another person, as I was still afraid of it, concerned about the consequences. The venom, however, flowed freely in the journal. There were no inhibitions or fears. The feelings were no threat to me, so I could feel them, express them, and remain unharmed by the process. What a huge relief!

My blood boils and I hate you
My feelings unfold and they are denied
My expression is negated
And where does that power go?

Beneath, beneath
Below, below
To boil and rumble from deep within
To catch you by surprise some other day,
　　　　　　　　　　　　some other time

As my friend the journal allowed me to work through my anger, as it gave me a place to vent and steam and rage, I became transformed and arrived at the next stage of grief, bargaining.

At first I could not come up with the "bargaining" stage of my process. Then I became aware of how I would do a little bit of grief work and then put it aside, wanting it to be healed. I had a difficult time with the process part. It was like making a deal: "Okay, grief, I'll work real hard in this one sitting, and then I want to be done with it. I want the pain to be over, and I want to be healed."

April 29　And ultimately I feel sad about having to deal with being sad. The never-ending cycle.

May 4　100 Things I Have Never Mourned, Grieved, Acknowledged Loss or Felt Sorry About. [List of 8 items follows.] This is dry and has no emotion at all. I think maybe I am tired. My heart is not in it and I don't feel like wasting my time trying to make it happen. I don't think it will serve to force it.

My pain and my grief
my sadness and my sorrow
are all a part of me

A valuable part of me
born from the essence
of my feelings.

Touching the raw nerves
of what I am

I feel!
I am touched by my experiences!
Nothing goes unnoticed!

How can I deprive myself
of the rights to my feelings

How can I shut my eyes
to all that I am

Others suffer

Let me suffer as well

The pulling in and letting go process of bargaining. One day willing, the next day finished, the day after open again. Push me, pull me, let me make a deal. It certainly has an aspect of control, but that's another chapter. Finally it got through to me that my bargaining was not working. I found I had to do the work to reap the rewards:

May 10   (Dialogue with Grief)

ME: How can I change, or handle you differently?

GRIEF: Acknowledge me and do everything in your
power to meet me head-on. Get through it.
Get beyond it. Do it.

And so with that bit of encouragement, I made a commitment to not leave it until I was through. I submitted to the flow
of time and knew that the issues and old pains would come up
as they needed to. I vowed to remain open to the continuing
process.

With bargaining out of the way, I was free to continue into
the next stage of grief, that of depression.

I recognized depression quickly. I have lived there for long
enough periods of time that I know it well.

May 14   I am really tired—and tired of being tired.

May 15   Haven't been writing much and I don't know
why. Partially I'm sure it's exhaustion. I'm tired of being
tired.

May 18   Having a really hard time getting up in the
morning. It's a struggle every day.

There was more to my depression than tiredness and lack of
"zip." Included was a lack of patience, a short attention span,
and a feeling of emptiness.

May 19   I'm wondering just what it is that is happening
to me, or perhaps more accurately what it is that I am
participating in completely unaware. I find myself drifting
through my days seemingly half-conscious. Having
strange lapses in mental ability and recall. Calling people
by the wrong name, forgetting simple things and eating
too much. None of which I take delight in.

THE FIVE STAGES OF GRIEF

I want to be left alone
and I am dying of aloneness

I wonder what part I play in life
and I really don't care

Everyone else in the world is a flaming idiot
and I know nothing

I want to scream and yell and moan
I want to quietly crawl in a hole and die

I have a million, trillion, zillion things that
   absolutely, positively must be done today
and there is no reason to get out of bed

Depression scares me terribly
and I love being in this familiar place

At this point I again must acknowledge my journal in the movement through these stages. Where would I have been without it? What a blessed gift. . . . What a joyous experience, and it is with me now as I move into acceptance.

Part of what I must accept is the fact that the grief model is not linear. I am not completely through with the first four stages, but I am closer to living in acceptance than I have ever experienced before. Once again, the journal mirrors that for me.

May 21   Layer after layer, closer and closer to the core. But it's not just painful; it is a life-giving process as well. . . . I am aware that it is when I try to protect myself from the pain that what I truly end up doing is shutting myself off from the wholeness of what life has to offer.

May 24   And though the struggle has been intense and at times has seemed unbearable, the gifts have been in equal proportion to the pain I seemed to have had to endure.

PUTTING IT ALL TOGETHER

May 27   100 Things I Am Grateful For
97. Joy
98. Sorrow
99. Joy
100. Myself

This feels like a pretty accurate metaphor for how it is. My joy surrounding the grief and sorrow on either side, and under it all is myself.

Would I have really had it any other way?
If I had to do it all again
Would I not grab the same things I've grabbed for?
Would I not choose the same paths I've chosen?
And hasn't it all been worth it?
Aren't I looking forward to what is on the
horizon?
Do I not know that my Soul loves me?

Thanks to my journal can never adequately be addressed. I have a true friend for life. I need one. I deserve one. I am eternally grateful.

21

HEALING CHILDHOOD WOUNDS THROUGH JOURNALING

by Edelle Kinsinger

Every childhood's conflictual experiences remain hidden and locked in darkness, and the key to our understanding of the life that follows is hidden away with them.

—Dr. Alice Miller
The Drama of the Gifted Child

I have often wondered at the dearth of memories available to me from my childhood. The few vivid images I carry of my early years are limited to experiences with nature. I can recall the details of picking up a tiny red snake by the tail and watching in horror as it broke in two, one half slithering through the grass, the other wriggling in my hand. This picture is clear, complete, with sounds, smells, and emotions intact.

Yet I have only vague, hazy impressions of long Minnesota winters spent indoors with my mother. What events and feelings filled my days and years in the lost time from birth to age 10?

Amnesia surrounding childhood is not unusual. The Swiss psychoanalyst Alice Miller reports that many adults are unable to remember their childhoods. According to Miller, these memories are repressed at a time when it is necessary for the child's emotional survival to forget. To experience the pain of wounds inflicted by parents on whom the child is totally dependent is, in the child's undeveloped mind, tantamount to death. And so the child learns not to feel—and eventually, not to remember—these hurts.

The repression often continues into adulthood, long after it has served its useful purpose of self-protection, and results in separation from the true self, denial of feelings, inability to attain intimacy with another person, and ultimately, depression.

"I had no memories at all of the first five years of my life, and even those of the following years were very sparse," writes Miller of her own experience. "Although this is an indication of strong repression—something that never occurs without good reason—it did not prevent me from clinging to the belief that my parents had provided me with loving care and made every effort to give me everything I needed as a child."

Thus, for many of us, the myth of a happy childhood replaces any recognition of truth. This myth also prevents any direct dealing with the wounds which run so deep that our Inner Child fears their lancing may result in emotional or physical death.

"Experience has taught us," Miller states in *The Drama of the Gifted Child*, "that we have one enduring weapon in our struggle against mental illness: The emotional discovery and emotional acceptance of the truth in the individual and unique history of our childhood."

In Miller's personal drama she was able to uncover repressed childhood wounds only when she began to paint. At the age of

45 she began to experiment with color and form for the first time. She reports that the playfulness of this experience led to some bitter images that she recognized as memories of a traumatic childhood. Painting opened the door for her to remember the pain, to bring it out in the open where she could allow her Adult Self to go to her Child Self and give the child everything she needed.

For me, this healing experience has taken place in the pages of my journal. Many of my journal entries feel like pure creative power, available like Miller's paintings to attest to the wounding of my Child Self, but available further to offer miraculous healing—healing which can only take place after the wound has been recognized, probed, and laid bare. For this, the art of journaling, in its infinite variety, is well suited.

My journal adventure was not a planned trip. In fact, the first step of my venture into my wounded childhood happened quite unexpectedly. After a particular heated argument with my teenage daughter, I wrote an imaginary Dialogue between us. I was struck by the viciousness of the attack she launched against me in the pages of my journal. The words poured forth in wanton destruction with such vehemence that I was forced to realize that these were not the words of my daughter but rather my own intense self-hatred spewing from my soul, laying bare my feelings of tremendous guilt and shame.

Continuing the Dialogue technique, I switched partners and wrote to my guilt, seeking desperately to understand:

ME: Guilt, you really are strong. I can't imagine how you got to be that big.

GUILT: You really fed me even when you were a kid. Everything bad that ever happened, you thought it was because of you. I think you probably thought your mom was so unhappy because of you.

ME: She always seemed like she couldn't stand
      one more thing.

This simple exchange between my guilt and me gave me
enough information to feel that perhaps my guilt was not as
totally inexplicable as I had thought. I concluded that perhaps
if I looked at my childhood with sensitivity and empathy for the
child who once was me, I would be able to gain insight into the
hurt I have always felt.

For as long as I can remember, my mother has been telling
me the story of her own unhappy childhood. This was a story I
knew well but had always sought to escape. Perhaps there was
some key to my own life in her story, I thought. And so I began
writing a descriptive essay in the third person relating her life
story as I remembered her telling it. Somewhere in the second
page of writing I automatically switched to writing in the first
person. I was no longer writing about "her," but rather about
"me." The essay turned into a journal entry written from an
altered point of view:

> She was a tough young woman. She learned fast, and if at
> all possible, she never let them know or see her ignorance.
> She met other farm girls who had come to the city for
> work. On weekends we might go to a dance or a movie. It
> was the first time I'd ever had any fun. I was always careful
> not to have too much fun. I knew how terrible it could all
> become.

In the writing somewhere, perhaps in the living somewhere,
her story became my story. The feeling of connection was so
intense that I immediately wrote a journal poem:

> mother
> or other
> cannot tell
> if the hell

was hers
or mine
where the line
divides our souls
in the flatlands
of my mind

It seemed that I had to recognize the connection, see our oneness, before I could work for separation. Out of this work on the life of my mother came a fragment of a childhood memory: a scene of walking to the bus stop with my mother in the winter when she was very tired, sick, and pregnant. I was three years old.

From this fragment of memory I wrote a journal entry dated March 1949. Using my journal as a time machine, I wrote as if I were again three years old, seeing my mother sick and sad and wanting desperately to make her happy. But no matter how hard I tried to be funny, good, helpful, or caring, I couldn't get through to her:

Mommy, look at me! Watch me twirl! Aren't I cute, Mommy? Don't you think I'm cute? I can run, Mommy! I can skip! Don't you think I skip nice? I can skip all the way to the bus stop! Can't you smile, Mommy? Can't you smile at the way I skip? Why can't I make you happy, Mommy? Aren't I cute enough?

The experience was powerful. Begun in my adult style of cursive handwriting, my script soon became the large, scrawled alphabet letters of a child. My thinking patterns also changed; I went from rational, adult awareness and comprehension to a child's illogical acceptance of complete responsibility for her mother's sadness. I rambled on in incessant pleading and bargaining in an attempt to make her happy. I was the child Alice Miller describes, offering to be the "well-behaved, reliable, empathetic, understanding and convenient child who in fact was never a child at all."

In just a few journal entries I learned that I had sacrificed my childhood at a very early age in order to take care of my mother. My parents fed this relationship constantly, and all the things they said to me all those years ago play over and over in my subconscious. For most of my life, I have struggled to keep these messages from my conscious awareness, for fear that I would be overpowered by them and actually believe their truth.

Armed with the power of my journal, though, I decided to bring these messages to light, trusting that conscious recognition would illuminate them and allow me to see them in their proper size and importance. I wrote a list of "100 Things My Parents Used to Say to Me." Each entry in the list was a separate little guilt trip.

For instance, as I neared adolescence I felt a natural internal desire to expand my awareness of the world around me. In my mind I could hear my parent's accusation as I would leave the house to explore: "What's the matter, aren't we good enough for you anymore?" Because their needs for security and unconditional acceptance were never met by their own parents, my mother and father needed me to constantly give them my undivided attention, my time, and my exclusive love.

I used the journal as time machine many times, writing Captured Moments from snatches of childhood memories, each time feeling that I had received a gift of understanding and each time feeling increased sympathy and identification with the confused, hurt, lonely, and frightened child.

A very powerful healing imagery came to me one day as I was writing and listening to a tape of a thunderstorm. In this imagery, my Adult Self went to my Inner Child and protected her. This imagery was prompted by the recollection of an actual thunderstorm many years ago when, as a child, I sought protection from an adult who instead sexually abused me. In my imagery, my own Adult Self gave the child everything she needed and asked nothing in return. I held her, warmed her, protected her, and finally led her away to her real home where the adults all treated each other, and especially the children, with great respect. Through the journal I was able to give my Inner Child exactly what she needed to heal the wounds and come out with respect and love.

The whole experience of opening to my feelings, recognizing them and participating in my own healing, has given me a new sense of inner power. And the next journal step to take emerges naturally each time. After the thunderstorm imagery, I needed a forum to express anger and deep rage at the people who hurt me as a child. The journal was a perfect receptacle for this rage. I began with a list of "100 Fantasies Which Are Not Suitable for Polite Company." The paper unconditionally accepted my deepest, darkest, most horrible thoughts. And the thoughts themselves lost their power simply through the light of awareness.

Even when the healing process is well under way or complete, the journal continues to be a valuable tool for self-processing. When the Inner Child has been listened to, taken seriously, allowed to hurt and to rage, the adult may be ready to make a healthy reconciliation with the parents who were themselves victims. The adult can see the tragedy in the cycle. The journal is available for this process, as the adult recognizes the true feelings of love for the parents. This love is not dependent on a myth of happiness but rather is based on openness and truth.

At this point, the journaler may experience the liberation of creativity, since the Inner Child is now free to express with complete acceptance. The journal allows the child to play with no rules and limitless possibilities for expression. No other method of therapy leaves us such a record of the journey, continually ready to be perused for further insight or simply as testament to how far we have come.

22
JOURNAL WRITING FOR ADULT CHILDREN OF ALCOHOLICS

by Cynthia Walser

When is a child not a child? When the child lives with alcoholism.

–Janet Geringer Woititz, Ed.D.
Adult Children of Alcoholics

Although each of us is unique—the situations, perceptions, and interpretations of our lives are individual—Adult Children of dysfunctional families often face similar tasks. These tasks include recognizing denial, releasing our pain, letting go of the need for control, and looking at the world realistically.

What better friend than the journal to help with these tasks? For it is an environment that can be created with safety and structure, an environment that is consistent, an environment that accepts the truth as we perceive it without criticism. The journal environment, in other words, shows a marked contrast to the environment in which the typical Adult Child grew up.

CAPTURED MOMENTS

A common thread in dysfunctional families is denial. When Daddy flew into an alcoholic rage and Mommy ignored him and went on cooking dinner, you received two distinctly different, and inconsistent, messages. Mommy may have even told you Daddy wasn't really mad. So whom do you believe? Daddy, who is shouting that nobody in the family loves him? Or Mommy, who is acting like nothing unusual is going on? And can you even trust yourself enough to believe your own experience?

This inconsistency in what you observed or directly experienced and what you were told is a very common story among Adult Children. It leads to profound confusion and a bizarre sense that you can't rely on your own perception. Captured Moments offer great value to Adult Children in that the writing can bring up and release denied or buried pain.

Writing Captured Moments can provide the clarity that is often missing when we try to make contact with our childhood. The following example demonstrates the intensity that can be wrought when writing from the eyes of the child you once were:

Sitting on the back step. The sounds of crickets as it begins to turn to darkness, the curtain closing over the warm sunny day. The cows moving towards the barn, bell tinkling—milking time—a comforting sound somehow, combined with their slow, steady pace.

"I wonder when he's going to get home?"

Legs crossed, fiddling with her hair, she waits.

"This time I'm really going to be mad and I'm going to tell him! I'll just sit out here all night and wait. He can't get past me—he's going to get it now!"

Her anger embraces her. She sees herself telling him

what she thinks, the unjustness of his actions. She begins to yell at him in her mind, then reasonable, carefully chosen words convince him of his foolishness. He asks for forgiveness and hugs her. He's home again and they go inside and greet her mother, his wife.

She just knows it could work that way. Then they'd all be happy again. They would laugh and go to the drive-in, all snuggly in their pj's. Mom and Dad in the front while she lay dozily in back with her brother and sister. . . .

Her mother comes out, tells her it is bedtime. She doesn't want to tell her mom why she is waiting—doesn't want to draw attention to her father, who isn't there, so reluctantly she walks inside, closing out the sound of the crickets. Reluctantly, she walks up the stairs. It's time to go to bed for another night.

The act of writing this Captured Moment released a barrage of intense and vivid feelings, and I realized that the pain associated with my father goes back to the time I was a small girl. It was through this journal entry that I began to see the control that I thought I could exercise as a child, as well as the attitude that it was my responsibility to "fix" my family and make it work. At the end of the story I was able to recognize that even as a child, I knew the futility in that attitude, yet I continued the scenario over and over, never giving up hope that I could change things.

This vignette touches upon another aspect of Captured Moments, that of insight into patterns established. When you write from the perspective of yourself as a child, you are able to see the types of attitudes and behaviors that you perceived as necessary for survival or security then. You can then compare those perceptions to your current situation to see if your habitual behavior is still appropriate or useful. In almost every instance, you'll find that it is not!

Through the following example, I realized my belief that I must use my will to make things all right. As this is a common characteristic of Adult Children (and particularly the subset known as Family Heroes), its realization was an important step in my recovery process:

She lay awake.

Not hearing the crickets, the muffled sounds of campers around unseen fires or the rhythmic breathing of her family, she only heard them laughing. The sound made her pull inward, grasping the sleeping bag to her, clenching her hands and eyelids tight.

"Why are they still out there? Why does he spend so much time with Uncle Jack? Who wanted him to come, anyway?" A waft of guilt as she cursed herself. Uncle Jack was a wonderful friend, held her on his lap, called her his "big girl." But now he was taking away her dad. Their family vacation was wrecked as they sat outside night after night, drinking beer and laughing.

Again she tried her will, willed them to come in, crawl in their sleeping bags, complete the warmth and security of the family sleeping. She clenched her eyes and willed, "Please come in, please love us, please, please show us that we are important, too."

She woke up and listened. No laughing, only the deep, steady breathing of slumber. Her body loosened. A sigh. Everything was okay now. They were all together for another night.

This entry, as well, brought up intense and painful feelings. I felt a deep sadness as I realized how subtly I was affected by my father's alcoholism. My father did not yell, hit, or come home raving drunk. He just didn't come home. And so writing of this time also triggered old abandonment fears. "I'm no longer dependent on my parents, or anyone, to live, yet the fear is right there as I write," I continued after the Captured Moment. "The fear of being left alone, unloved."

CHARACTER SKETCH

In the beginning, when you are first starting to look and perhaps to see, Character Sketches can be useful tools.

It may be useful to write a sketch of a drinking parent, both at the times of drinking and times of sobriety. It is important to acknowledge the often varying aspects of the parent; Character Sketches can help point out the dramatic shifts.

As an Adult Child, one of your tasks will be to identify the patterns that you are carrying with you into adulthood. These patterns are often expressed in intimate relationships. Therefore, it is also useful to write Character Sketches of partners, spouses, employers, and intimate friends. Similarities, differences, projections, "hidden" characteristics, patterns, and perceptions will surface.

UNSENT LETTER

Writing a letter to an alcoholic parent or another member of the dysfunctional family can be a powerfully freeing experience, especially when you allow yourself to be totally unencumbered, without the restrictions created by a fear of the reaction of the recipient. It is an opportunity to release the anger and frustration that was not expressed in childhood because of the state of dependency.

It's helpful when writing an Unsent Letter to completely let go, to not worry about being nice. This is an opportunity to let all that hurt and resentment out, unrestrained. I've found

Unsent Letters to be a wonderful way to rant and rave, be irrational, and clear the decks for a more effective discourse.

It was following such an Unsent Letter that the following "sent" letter was written, demonstrating the possibility of using an Unsent Letter to put down thoughts in such a way as to clarify to yourself where you stand.

Dear Dad,

I've always felt close to you—an admiration and appreciation of your view of life and interaction in it. You look at the good in things and have taught me about life's abundance. You've also made some mistakes, and some of those mistakes have hurt me very much. They've stayed with me, and they limit the love I feel for you as well as the love I share with others.

I'm afraid of writing this letter because of the hurt it may cause you. I feel like you've gone through a lot of hurt and I don't want to create more. But that feeling of betrayal and unfairness is still there. . . .

I'm realizing that I'm still very, very angry with you for not being totally there for us when we were kids. I have this image of waiting for you on the back steps—waiting for you to come home so I could yell at you—tell you how it wasn't fair that you were gone so late all of the time. I felt that somehow I could convince you to be home more, love us more, and we could be a happy family again.

Dammit, I felt like I had to be perfect. I know it's not rational, but I still think that way sometimes. And I don't want to be perfect. I just want to be able to be me, and you be you and not feel afraid or responsible or angry.

I want to let it go, but I don't want to pretend that it's all okay. I know it's in the past, but I still want to talk about it, to understand, to reconnect. Maybe when I come home we can take some time and do that. Can we? I love you.

CLUSTERING

Clustering allows our minds to "go" and associations to take place. Try choosing words to Cluster with that "push your buttons." For Adult Children of Alcoholics, these may include:

- perfectionist
- drunk
- "no problem"
- denial
- helpless
- booze

The following journal entry resulted from a Cluster around the word "afraid." The writing led to further explorations of the origins and results of the fear:

Afraid, alone.
  All of my fears, my feeling afraid, originate with aloneness. Isolation, nonacceptance, not being loved, manifest as fears of physical hurt, rejection for my actions or decisions. Ultimate aloneness.
  Funny—fearing, I become apprehensive, closed to people and to joy.
  I become afraid and alone.

TRANSFORMING LIMITATIONS

During the healing and growing process, it is important to acknowledge progress and to participate in the beauty of life as well as the struggles. The following techniques are useful in facilitating these processes.

Sometimes when we are dealing with issues, we become immersed in those issues and don't see beyond them. Lists of 100 ("Things I Feel Confident About," "Ways I've Grown," "Joys in My Life") can remind us of the abundance and positive aspects of our lives in a powerful way.

Another way to see the possibilities of abundance in our lives is to transform the perception of limitations into affirmations. This reinforces a perception of self-responsibility. One role often taken on by Adult Children is that of victim; we see things happening "to" us rather than taking responsibility for ourselves in the situation. Writing of our fears, insecurities, and beliefs that are limiting, and then transforming them into affirmations is an act of self-empowerment. This act can be seen as a reflection of the action we are able to take in our lives. For example:

LIMITATIONS	AFFIRMATIONS
I am afraid of abandonment	I am strong and capable
If I'm not nice, people won't love me	I'm lovable and can be appreciated just the way I am
I must be perfect	I am allowed to make mistakes
I must do it all myself	I can ask for help
I have to pretend to know all the answers	It's okay to feel confused
I must always keep my "mask" in place	My vulnerability is part of my humanness

OTHER TECHNIQUES

Dialogues, Perspectives, Steppingstones . . . virtually all journal techniques can be adapted for the special needs and tasks of Adult Children. The journal can be invaluable in the process of recovery, providing a compilation of awareness as well as a synopsis of the path traveled. The journal can be the perfect vehicle to help the hurt and lonely child inside grow up into a healthy, happy adult.

SECTION IV
THE ROAD GOES EVER ON

▼

INTRODUCTION

The Road goes ever, on and on
Down from the door where it began
Now far ahead the Road has gone
And I must follow, if I can
Pursuing it with eager feet
Until it joins some larger way
Where other paths and byways meet.
And whither then? I cannot say.

—J. R. R. Tolkien
The Fellowship of the Ring

And so we come to the end of our travels together. I thank you for inviting me to guide you; I hope you, too, have grown.

I leave you, then, to journey as you will, knowing that when your journal travels with you, you have your Self for company. Should you desire traveling companions, consider taking a journal class or workshop in your area, or find a few friends and start a journal support group.

I welcome your inquiries, sharings, and feedback. Please write me at this address:

THE ROAD GOES EVER ON

The Center for Journal Therapy
P.O. Box 19858
Denver, CO 80219

In parting, I offer this blessing:

May the starlight of time be on your side
May the winds of eternity be forever yours
And Godspeed in your endeavor,
For a lot of ground there is to cover.

SUGGESTED
READING

JOURNAL WRITING

Baldwin, Christina. *One to One: Self-Understanding through Journal Writing*. New York: M. Evans & Co., 1977. One of the first books available for the mass market on journal therapy. Many examples come from the author's own diaries.

Biffle, Christopher. *The Castle of the Pearl*. Barnes & Noble Books, 1983. A delightful Guided Imagery fantasy in which you become both the creator and the main character.

Cappachione, Lucia. *The Creative Journal*. Athens: Swallow

Press, 1979. A combination of art/process journal instruction with approximately 50 exercises to play with.

————. *The Power of Your Other Hand.* North Hollywood: Newcastle Publishing, 1988. How writing with the non-dominant hand can free up creativity and the voice of the Inner Child.

Daniel, Lois. *How to Write Your Own Life Story.* Chicago: Chicago Review Press, 1985. An excellent step-by-step approach to autobiographical writing.

Goldberg, Natalie. *Writing Down the Bones.* Boston: Shambala, 1986. A delightful romp through one woman's approach to writing as a "discipline" similar to meditation or yoga.

Hagan, Kay Leigh. *Internal Affairs: A Journalkeeping Workbook for Self-Intimacy.* Atlanta: Escapadia Press, 1988. A beautiful and inviting workbook to experiment with self-reflective writing.

Progoff, Ira. *At a Journal Workshop.* New York: Dialogue House, 1975. The text for the famous Intensive Journal Workshop.™ Dr. Progoff is widely acknowledged to be the founder of the journal therapy movement.

————. *The Practice of Process Meditation.* New York: Dialogue House, 1981. The text for the meditation (purple) section of the Intensive Journal.™

Rainer, Tristine. *The New Diary.* Los Angeles: J. P. Tarcher, 1978. How to use a journal for self-guidance and expanded creativity. A simply marvelous book.

Rico, Gabriele Lusser. *Writing the Natural Way.* Los Angeles: J. P. Tarcher, 1983. Right-brain techniques for the release of creative powers.

Simons, George F. *Keeping Your Personal Journal.* New York: Ballantine/Epiphany, 1978. Part I is a review of the basics. Part II, "Exploring Soul Country," contains insightful exercises to try.

JOURNAL READING

There are hundreds of published diaries and journals available. Check the "Biography" section of your favorite bookseller, or look under "Diaries" or "Journals" in your library. The following are some of my favorites:

Jung, Carl Gustav. *Memories, Dreams and Reflections.* Edited by Aniela Jaffe. New York: Vintage Books (Random House), 1961.The autobiography of this leader in the field of transpersonal psychology is rich with the symbology of his own inner life.

The Kensington Ladies' Erotica Society. *Ladies' Home Erotica.* Berkeley: Ten Speed Press, 1984. The fruits of a writing group which limited subject matter to a woman's view of sensuality and eroticism.

Moffat, Mary Jane, and Painter, Charlotte, eds. *Revelations: Diaries of Women.* New York: Vintage Books (Random House), 1975. A fascinating anthology of excerpts from the diaries of the famous, the semifamous, and the unknown.

Nin, Anäis. *The Diary of Anäis Nin.* 7 vols. Orlando: Harcourt Brace Jovanovich, 1966–1974. Nin virtually single-handedly vaulted the diary to its status as legitimate literature through the publication of her intense, intricate, and fascinating diaries.

Sarton, May. *Journal of a Solitude; At Seventy;* and others. New York: W. W. Norton, 1973, 1984. The journals of one of America's best-loved novelists and poets paint a rich portrait of life in her later years.

Stevens, Barry. *Don't Push the River.* Moab, Utah: Real People Press, 1970. The journal of one of Fritz Perls's students and close associates gives a fascinating look at the development of Gestalt psychotherapy.

OVERCOMING ADDICTIONS

Friends in Recovery. *The 12 Steps: A Way Out*. San Diego: Recovery Publications, 1987. Focuses on Adult Children issues with directions on setting up and running a Step Study Writing Workshop.

Latimer, Jane Evans. *Living Binge-Free: A Personal Guide to Victory Over Compulsive Eating*. Boulder: LivingQuest, 1988. A former bulimic provides a guide, including journal writing, out of the twisted maze of obsessive/compulsive eating.

McConnell, Patty. *A Workbook for Healing: Adult Children of Alcoholics*. New York: Harper & Row, 1986. A compassionate guide to recovery by one who has been there, using art, imagery, and structured exercises.

Roth, Geneen. *Feeding the Hungry Heart*. New York: New American Library, 1982. Journal entries illustrate her points on understanding and overcoming compulsive overeating.

Woititz, Janet Geringer. *Adult Children of Alcoholics*. Pompano Beach: Health Communications, 1983. One of the first books published for and about ACAs, it has become a classic in the field.

DREAMWORK

Kaplan-Williams, Strephon. *The Jungian-Senoi Dreamwork Manual*. Berkeley: Journey Press, 1980. Perhaps the most comprehensive do-it-yourself guide to Jungian dreamwork.

Reid, Clyde H. *Dreams: Discovering Your Inner Teacher*. San Francisco: Harper & Row, 1983. A guidebook packed with helpful ideas for self-discovery through dreamwork.

Ullman, Montague, and Nan Zimmerman. *Working with*

Dreams. Los Angeles: J. P. Tarcher, 1979. A good basic text for dream appreciation and understanding.

SPECIAL INTEREST

Bolen, Jean Shinoda. *The Tao of Psychology: Synchronicity and the Self*. San Francisco: Harper & Row, 1979. An exploration of the hidden messages and deeper significance of what Jung called "meaningful coincidence."

Ellis, Normandi. *Awakening Osiris: The Egyptian Book of the Dead*. Grand Rapids: Phanes Press, 1988. This new translation, made from the hieroglyphs, approaches the Book of the Dead as a profound spiritual text for our time and reads like pure, diaphanous verse.

Keyes, Margaret Frings. *Inward Journey: Art as Therapy*. La Salle: Open Court Publishing, 1983. How art journals can uncover clues to the psyche.

Klauser, Henriette Anne. *Writing on Both Sides of the Brain*. New York: Harper & Row, 1987. For all who must write but think they can't. This book is warm, it is witty, it is wise; best of all, it *works*.

Miller, Alice. *The Drama of the Gifted Child*. Translated by Ruth Ward. New York: Basic Books, 1981. Based on Dr. Miller's work with regaining the capacity for genuine feelings, which is the source of natural vitality.

————. *Pictures of a Childhood*. Translated by Hildegaarde Hannam. New York: Farrar, Straus & Giroux, 1986. Reproductions of Dr. Miller's artistic journey into the depths of her own painful past.

Sher, Barbara. *Wishcraft: How to Get What You Really Want*. New York: Ballantine Books, 1979. Effective strategies for making real change in your life.

ABOUT THE AUTHOR

Kay Adams is a psychotherapist and internationally recognized pioneer in the field of journal therapy. She has designed and trained journal writing programs in the United States and Canada since 1985 and travels extensively to consult on the use of reflective writing as a therapeutic tool.

She is the journal therapist for The National Center for the Treatment of Dissociative Disorders in Denver, Colorado.

Through The Center for Journal Therapy, Kay certifies instructors for the JOURNAL TO THE SELF workshop and offers journal therapy conferences and trainings.

She is presently working on her second book for Warner, MIGHTIER THAN THE SWORD: THE JOURNAL AS A PATH TO MEN'S SELF-DISCOVERY.

For information about workshops, consultations, instructor certification, or Kay's quarterly newsletter, please write or fax:

Kathleen Adams, M.A.
The Center for Journal Therapy
P.O. Box 963
Arvada, CO 80001
FAX 303-421-1255